IT'S WORTH IT 2.0

Discovering God's Plan for You in
a Place You Might Not *Expect*

JEFF LITTLE

It's Worth It 2.0 is dedicated to the faithful people of Milestone Church who give, serve, and love others with a desire to honor Jesus.

Outside of my family, my greatest joy is being your pastor. You make this responsibility a gift and a privilege. I would not trade it for anything in the world.

THANK YOU,
JEFF LITTLE, DMin

TABLE O
CONTEN

Why Do We Need *It's Worth It 2.0?*

You may be familiar with the first book I wrote, *It's Worth It.* Maybe you've had the chance to read it. Maybe it's been on the shelf and you've been meaning to get to it.

So you're probably wondering, *why do we need a 2.0?* That's a great question.

A lot has changed since I wrote it. Our world has shifted. A global pandemic was a major disruption for families, schools, businesses, and churches. It forced each of these environments to evaluate their strategies and working models.

The landscape of the church has changed. Over the years I've developed some new relationships with mentors and friends who are a little further down the road. I've also continued to grow closer to long-standing relationships with trusted leaders and we've all realized how critical it is that we continue to clarify our values and our mission in order to serve people well.

Our church has grown significantly. We've added campuses. Our team also consistently serves other churches because we're honored to be part of the body of Christ and what God is doing. In the process of serving churches, we've gained new perspectives and insights.

I've grown and changed since I wrote the first book. In addition to all the new opportunities for growth, I've written several other books. I've always valued personal development and education, and I recently completed my Doctor of Ministry degree.

In all of these ventures I have been propelled by one thought: *How can I serve and lead you better? I want you to grow.*

And so here we are—*It's Worth It 2.0.* My best estimate is that *this book is 85% new content.* Our values haven't changed and some of the concepts and insights may sound familiar if you've read my other books. But what started as an update ended up as a new book for a new season in an attempt to better serve and lead our church family.

I am more excited than ever about what God is doing in the body of Christ, in Milestone Church, and in you.

INTRODUCTION

THE BIBLE IS FILLED WITH STORIES. Some are long; some are short. Some are easy to understand; others are mysterious.

Jesus was such a great storyteller—He could tell a story in one verse. Two sentences. Thirty-five words. But this story is still being told thousands of years later.

> *The kingdom of heaven is like treasure hidden in a field. When a man found it, he hid it again, and then in his joy went and sold all he had and bought that field.*[1]

A man is walking through a field. We don't know his name; we don't know anything about him. All we know is that when he finds the treasure, he hides it, and then he sells everything he has to buy the field.

---

[1] Matthew 13:44

It looks like dirt. It's easy to miss. Most people who walk past a field of dirt don't even notice. They don't pay attention because it's not a big deal.

But when you find the treasure, you sell everything it takes in order to get it.

The only detail Jesus gives us about this man's emotional state of mind is his joy. He's not anxious or nervous about the deal. He is thrilled. He has no buyer's remorse. It feels too good to be true.

There is no doubt in his mind this treasure is worth everything he has.

The irony of this little sentence is that we can't buy what Jesus is offering—He gives it freely. It's not cheap, but He's the One who pays the price.

Jesus tells this story to give us a picture of what it's like to be included in the Kingdom of heaven. I realize this is one of those things in the Bible that's not clear. Is the Kingdom of heaven . . . heaven? Like the place with clouds, robes, and streets of gold?

It's actually better than that.

This story is from the Gospel of Matthew, which was primarily addressed to a Jewish audience. One of the ways they showed reverence to God was to not say His name. Unlike the other Gospels, Matthew primarily uses this phrase to describe God's Kingdom.

The idea that the Kingdom of God had come to Earth was the main message Jesus preached. It's what He told His disciples to preach when He sent them out. The Kingdom was not another way to describe a religion or a personal decision to become more spiritual.

When Jesus said God's Kingdom had come, and His will would be done on Earth as it is in heaven, He was saying, through Him, God was making everything on Earth the way He wanted it to be. [2]

What would you give to be included in that? You'd give everything you have, and everything you would ever have, to be included in the place where God's peace and His presence filled your life.

We hope this is true. We want this to be true. But it can be hard to believe.

In so many places in life, we want treasure and we end up with dirt.

- *The mom who sacrifices everything to meet her kids' every need, who prays for them tirelessly, who gives generously, who teaches patiently…and still feels like she didn't do enough.*
- *The student who wants to be included and valued by their peers, who finally makes it to the "in crowd," only to discover they don't like who they've become.*
- *The couple who checks Zillow on a daily basis, looks at hundreds of listings, saves, waits patiently, writes the best letter to stand out over all the offers…and gets their dream house! But after six months, their marriage isn't doing great, the kids are struggling, and they ask themselves, was it worth it?*

[2] You may recognize this from the Lord's Prayer in Matthew 6:10.

- *The career person who works extra hours, closes the record deal, pushes for the dream promotion through rounds of interviews…and finally gets it. The newfound respect is great, the salary increase is awesome, but if they're honest, they liked their previous role better. The people and the work were more fulfilling.*
- *The young adult who waited patiently as everyone in their friend group found their special someone. They wondered if it would ever happen for them. And then…finally! But after a few weeks of marriage, they secretly wonder, "Is it this hard for everyone? Why am I not happier?"*
- *The empty nester who pushed hard for early retirement and hit all their targets in order to spend time with their family and prioritize their grandkids…only to be blindsided by significant family tension over unclear expectations.*

These are just a few scenarios of the countless ways we're promised every day that if we can just get "this," then all of our dreams will come true. It drives our economy. It captures our attention. But ultimately it lets us down.

I could give you many more scenarios, but I think you get the point. And this doesn't take into account all of life's curveballs:

- *The sickness you don't see coming*
- *The failure of a business*
- *The loss of a job*
- *The end of a marriage*
- *The isolation and loneliness*

In these moments, it's easy to feel like life is only dirt. There is no treasure. The world keeps promising other solutions if we just try harder. There's never been a time in history when we've been more aware of what everyone else has and what everyone is doing.

It's like our lives have become a constant advertisement for all the ways we're missing out. We've never had more. We've never needed so many storage units to hold the stuff we don't even have space for. We've never been more anxious. We've never had more options.

And yet most people live with way more dirt than treasure. They would say they don't have as much joy as they'd like.

God has something better for us, but it's in a place we might not expect.

I wrote this book because I want you to find the treasure.

I wrote this book because I want to help you find the ways to look past the dirt in order to find the treasure.

I believe Jesus was inviting each and every one of us to share the experience of the man in this little story. I believe that in these thirty-five words we can find help discovering the life we were created to live.

I believe Jesus has so much treasure for each of us; we just have to learn how to find it. To the untrained eye, it can look like dirt.

- I believe He has treasure for us through divine re-lationships—people God places into our lives who will love and support us.

- I believe He has treasure for us as we grow into the person He created us to be. When we discover the unique gifts and talents He has given us, we find genuine fulfillment through using those gifts to serve others.
- I believe He has treasure for us as He invites us to be part of something bigger than ourselves and a place where we belong.

But I'm getting ahead of myself.

Let me simply say it this way:

There is no treasure greater
than Jesus Himself.

I don't know what you think about Him. I'm not sure what you've heard. I've given my life to help people see Him for who He really is.

Maybe someone told you that to be a Christian is to work really hard, to do as many spiritual things as possible, and to keep a record of all the ways everyone else has blown it so that when you die, God will think you're a good person.

I know a lot of people think that's the message of Jesus. It's not. And it's a pretty miserable way to live.

Maybe someone told you you're basically a good person. We're all good people. As long as we try our best, and allow everyone else to believe whatever they want to believe, then all spiritual approaches and paths are essentially the same. We're free to follow our own hearts, as long as we don't hurt other people. It sounds so kind.

The problem is, deep down, we know it's not true. We do things we're not proud of. We hurt the people we love. We feel guilty because we know we make mistakes.

And if we've made enough of them, we don't need any help to feel bad. We're good at beating ourselves up. We feel like we've blown it. We feel like we're on the outside. We feel unworthy.

Maybe someone told you there is no God. It's all made up. Religion is something weak-willed people need. It probably made sense to you for a moment. But when you stopped to think about it, if life was really about being the strongest and the smartest, then why aren't those people the most fulfilled? Are we all destined to be miserable? What a depressing way to live.

If the people who accomplished the most were the best versions of humanity and we should model our lives after them, then how do we explain the impact of Jesus?

It doesn't make sense. Why would an unmarried carpenter, who never had a family, never started a Fortune 500 company, was never elected to a political office, and never ruled a political kingdom, inspire the devotion of billions of people around the world thousands of years after He died?

Here's how I would explain it: Jesus is exactly who He says He is. He is the Son of God who takes away the sin of the world. He lived the perfect life we should live but are not able to. And

He died the death we all deserve in our place—not to condemn us, but to set us free.

He doesn't ask us to be perfect like Him in order to accept us. He makes the first move. On our worst day, at our lowest moment, when we are the furthest from God, He draws near to us. More than that…He's drawing us near to Him. That's what He does.

He could have stayed in heaven and demanded we rise up to be with Him. None of us would have ever made it. There's no ladder big enough for us to climb to Him.

So He came down to us. He humbled Himself, became a man, to show us what God is like and to bring us home. In His own words, He didn't come for the healthy; He came for the sick. The truth is, outside of Him, we're all sick.

One of my favorite verses in the Bible, 2 Corinthians 5:21, explains it this way: *"God made him who had no sin to be sin for us so that in him we might become the righteousness of God."*

It's the great exchange. He takes on our sin and gives us His perfect relationship, His perfect "right-standing" with God.

He didn't come for those who had it all figured out. He came to seek and save those who were lost. If you've ever felt like the whole church thing doesn't make sense, it's okay. Maybe you felt like you didn't come from the right family; you made too many mistakes; if anyone knew what you've done or what you've thought, they wouldn't accept you.

That's not how Jesus sees us.

He comes to us in love. He stands at the door of our hearts. He asks to come in and waits patiently. And to those who receive Him, He exchanges our brokenness for His peace. He takes our shame and gives us His joy. He welcomes us into the family of God, not on the basis of our merit, but through the free gift He offers to us.

If it sounds too good . . . it is. That's why this message of Jesus has been called "the Godspell"—the good story. It is a good story. It's the Greatest Story Ever Told. It takes the whole Bible to tell the story. Every book, every chapter, every verse, they point to the person of Jesus.

We couldn't get to God, so God came to us through Jesus. The Greek word is *evangelion*. It means "good news." We call it the gospel.

It's not "try hard to be a good person." That's not good news. The gospel is not how bad people get better when they try hard. The good news of the gospel is that dead people come back to life.

There is no news like it. It's worth everything we have. It's a treasure unlike any other.

And it's available to you.

Here's my disclaimer: You're only going to care about the things in this book if you love Jesus. He's the real treasure. He's the One who can show you what's really worth it.

He has so much for you. I hope you'll keep reading with me and find it for yourself.

SECTION 01

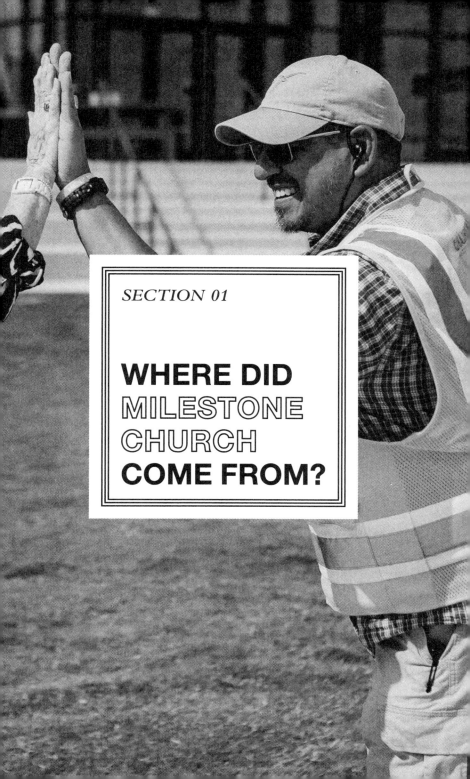

WHERE DID MILESTONE CHURCH COME FROM?

1

WE WANT
MORE FOR YOU
THAN FROM YOU

AS YOU START THIS BOOK, here is the simple prayer I'm praying for you: *Lord, help every person who reads these words to see what you see when you talk about this treasure. And not only would they see it, but would they experience it for themselves.*

My hope is that this becomes more than a book about church—I want it to really help you in the things you are concerned with on a daily basis.

This desire is at the very heart of Milestone Church. We like to say, "We want more for you than we want from you." It may seem hard to believe, but we mean it.

We really believe God sees you and knows the most intimate details of your life. That thing keeping you up late at night? He knows. That situation that you can't seem to change no matter how hard you try? He sees it.

He doesn't just see it—He's working on it, even when you can't see it.

He can be trusted. He is a good God who loves you more than you realize. Right now, even in this very moment, He is working to draw you closer to Him.

God sees you and knows the most intimate details of your life.

Life has always been challenging. Every generation has their own unique set of challenges and circumstances they are forced to contend with. We live in a complicated world with so many moving parts.

Most people I know are carrying a wide variety of concerns and responsibilities, and they live with this tension: *when one area of their lives begins to live up to their hopes, trouble pops up in another area.* Sound familiar? You are not alone.

We want to have a successful career, but we also want it to be meaningful and significant.

We want our income and lifestyle to continue to grow, but we also want to be fulfilled.

We want to meet the right person to spend the rest of our life with, but after watching all of our friends from college get married, we wonder if it will ever happen for us.

We want our kids to navigate through all the challenges of culture, to excel at something they're passionate about, and to become the best version of the people God created them to be.

But most of the time we feel like we're just trying to get them to do what we've asked them to do 15 times in the last 3 days. If we're really honest, we're not sure we know what to do or say to ensure their success.

This scares us, because there is nothing we want more. And most of us don't want to admit we feel this way.

We want genuine, authentic friendships—people who know the real us, love us, encourage us when we're down, and are there to celebrate life's biggest moments.

But we're not sure where to find these people, or how to hold on to them once they come into our lives. Sometimes the moment we find these types of relationships, we end up drifting apart, not because they stopped caring, but because the circumstances of our lives changed.

All of a sudden, we feel alone. We wonder where or how we'll find that kind of friendship again.

We want to grow closer to God, but we're not sure how that works, and we feel a little embarrassed to ask for help. It's hard to admit we don't really get it.

I realize we jumped into the deep end of the pool. These are the things we care about. I can write this with confidence because I care about each of these things too.

We care about these things because God created us for these things.

Significance and fulfillment, a relationship with our spouse that grows stronger and healthier over time, watching our children becoming who God called them to be, meaningful and life-giving friendships, and a dynamic relationship with God—these are the kinds of things that mark a truly exceptional life.

Those are the good days. But life also has the other moments. The challenge you didn't see coming that you know you're not strong enough to handle. Health scares, financial problems, relational conflicts . . . they come to each of our lives.

When you walk with God you begin to realize none of these are an indication He's left us or He doesn't care. Often in these moments, we recognize the depth of His love and the brilliance of His purpose in ways we never expected.

Here is the crazy part: I believe God wants this for every single person on the face of the earth. More than that, I believe God wants it for you.

You might be thinking, *Jeff, I thought this was a book about church.* Church may be the last thing you think about when you wonder how you can experience this kind of life. I get it. When people hear the word "church," I realize all kinds of things come to their mind, and many of them are not helpful.

But what if our connection to a church could actually help us experience this kind of life? What if God thinks the church is the best place to find it?

What if it was the only place to find it? How important would it be to tell people who had no idea?

I pastor a church in the Dallas/Fort Worth Metroplex. We live in a place where hundreds of thousands of people are moving from all over the world in search of better opportunities for their families and their careers. They're looking for a better life—and we're praying they find the life God created them to live.

As a church family, we feel a responsibility to help them find the treasure buried in the field. Because once you discover it, you will do whatever it takes to keep it. And you will want everyone you love to experience it too.

When people experience this treasure, it changes them. For years we've set aside a day where the whole church comes together to show the love of God in a practical way in our region. We call it "Serve Day." When we first started we had a few hundred people come together to complete about a dozen projects. We saw the impact right away—not only in the lives of the people who received the help, but also in the ones who served. They felt closer to God. They felt His love for people. They felt a deeper connection to their neighbors.

At the time I'm writing this, we recently held another Serve Day. This time it was several thousand people working on projects from our three different campuses in the Dallas/Fort Worth area.

Our teams cleared city code violations, they built beds for children who didn't have one, they installed ramps for veterans, they served those experiencing homelessness, and they completed hundreds of projects.

Why would they do this? Because they wanted someone else to find what they've found—the love and hope that come from a genuine relationship with Jesus.

I'm consistently amazed by this. In the few years surrounding the pandemic in 2020, I wondered if this might hinder our church's ability to continue to serve this way. The opposite happened. We found more ways to give.

When a massive ice storm hit our region, the people of Milestone mobilized to deliver firewood and water to those in need. They delivered dehumidifiers to families who had pipes burst. They delivered supplies to senior centers.

The response was so great, the city of Keller made Milestone Church the designated drive-thru location for anyone who needed water . . . and we gave away 5,500 cases of water! Through this radical act of love more than 25,000 people were impacted.

When a person receives this kind of help from someone who genuinely cares about them, it makes an impression—even if they have suspicions and doubts about church. They think, *Maybe there's something I missed.*

This is how we think about church—not as a religious organization doing irrelevant activities, but as a family of people demonstrating the love of God in a way that impacts those around them.

From the very beginning, this was our prayer for Milestone. We wanted to make a difference in the lives of real people. We wanted the cities we were located in to care that we were there. It has often been said that the church is the only entity

THIS IS HOW WE THINK ABOUT CHURCH—NOT AS A RELIGIOUS ORGANIZATION DOING IRRELEVANT ACTIVITIES, BUT AS A FAMILY OF PEOPLE DEMONSTRATING THE LOVE OF GOD IN A WAY THAT IMPACTS THOSE AROUND THEM.

that exists for its non-members. I love that idea.

In fact, it's more than an idea to me because I have seen what happens when a single mom comes to church for the first time nervous about how people will receive her. I have seen how overwhelmed and loved she feels when she realizes the person sitting next to her is honored to have her there. They've been praying and hoping she would come. They want both her and her kids to feel seen and loved.

THIS IS MORE THAN A RELIGIOUS GATHERING— IT'S A SPIRITUAL FAMILY.

I believe this moves the heart of God. I also believe people can sense and feel the presence of God when this happens.

And not just single moms, but people in their 40s who've never been to church before, people from different faith traditions, teens whose parents not only won't come with them but don't want them to go to church either, and empty nesters who begrudgingly come to church because their grandkids invited them.

This is more than a religious gathering— it's a spiritual family.

I don't know about you, but I'm grateful for the moms and grandmas who prayed us into the Kingdom of God. Before we were ready, when we weren't searching for God, when we didn't see the point, they faithfully prayed for us to experience the presence of God.

I had one of those moms.

She got up early every morning and read her Bible. I knew she had been there because by the time I stumbled into the kitchen I saw the ring on the napkin where her coffee mug had been. Morning by morning, she met God in His Word and prayed her heart out.

And because she did, my life was changed.

All these years later, I remember those coffee rings because they left a mark. The image of the lasting mark was instrumental in how we named our church.

Those coffee rings also told a story—a story of a mom who loved me enough to pray for me every morning. She prayed and asked God to get a hold of my life—that I'd answer the call and pursue the purpose He had for me. And for me to become the man, the husband, and the father He wanted me to be.

We approach church as a family. When people come to Milestone, they often say, "Everyone is so friendly. Where did you find all these amazing people?"

We believe there are so many great churches doing incredible things for God. We are honored just to be a part of the body of Christ. But we love who God has called us to be. We think approaching church like a family changes the way people feel when they come into our environment.

Learning from What You've Told Us

We've always wanted to help people get connected and see people take their next step. When you come to a new place, you don't want to feel like you stick out. You don't want to have to ask how to find friends and find a place to feel like you're part of what's happening. If there's no clear plan, a lot of us simply withdraw because we don't want to push through the awkwardness of not knowing how it works.

Don't get overwhelmed; just take your next step.

Our goal is not to pressure you or come on too strong, but we also know connection isn't automatic. Whenever we go to a new place, it helps to have someone help us get acclimated. We've learned so much throughout this process. We've changed a bunch of things. The people going through the process have been so helpful because as the church has grown, we've had to continually evaluate how to maintain our approach.

Repeatedly, we hear things like "This feels like home. It's so warm. I feel welcomed. I feel God here." We didn't want to lose this. I want to show you a few of the things that make up this culture. And I've also learned how rare it is for these three approaches to work together.

We think **it starts with *intentionality*.** We believe it's important to have a clear vision, to make things simple, to carefully think through why we do what we do. If we're not careful, church can be nebulous and vague—no one knows what we're trying to do or why we should care. We're not trying to make people feel bad for what they don't know. Our goal is to communicate in a way where everyone sees the *why* behind the *what* and knows what we're trying to do.

This is followed by *authenticity*. We believe it's critical to be genuine and approachable, to talk about how a relationship with God impacts our everyday lives in ways that real people with real problems can relate to. We're not trying to answer questions no one is asking. We're not trying to reach one kind of person. We're trying to reach all kinds of people—we're a multi-ethnic, multi-generational church. And we believe it's really hard to do this without being honest and genuine.

And the final ingredient is *sincerity*. It's possible to be intentional and authentic without the right motivation. However, we want to be motivated by a sincere love for people. Throughout the letters to the churches in the New Testament, we see this appeal to demonstrate genuine, sincere love for people.[1] Our primary motivation is the love of God. We're doing this for Jesus. We believe how we love and serve people is a direct reflection of how we love God.

We're not perfect, but we're doing our best to continue to become more and more of who God created us to be. No pretense or

[1] For example, 1 Peter 1:22 (NLT): "You were cleansed from your sin when you obeyed the truth so now you must show sincere love to one another as brothers and sisters. Love each other deeply with all your heart."

dishonesty. Dishonesty is frustrating in any organization, but it's tragic when it happens in church.

As you make your way through this book, my prayer is that God would show you the incredible treasures we find only in His Kingdom, which is expressed through His Church. Maybe this is a new idea for you. But despite the obstacles, I believe it really is worth it.

The Bible, spiritual family, His mission, discipleship, generosity— these are all treasures that build an exceptionally meaningful life. Not a life without challenges, but the life that truly is *life*.

The life we were created to live.

KEY THOUGHTS

- God sees you and knows the most intimate details of your life.

- Every human being wants to live a meaningful life, we want to find the right person to spend the rest of our lives with, we want our kids to reach their potential, and we want to know God because we are created for these things. But too often we don't know how to actually do it.

- God wants you to experience the best possible version of your life.

- The church is not a religious organization but God's family in the earth.

- We've built our church family around intentionality (clear plan), authenticity (genuine and approachable), and sincerity (no pretense or dishonesty).

NEXT STEPS

—As you make your way through the book, take a pen and write down what comes to mind in the margin. I'm hoping to spark questions and thoughts to help you grow.

2
WHEN THINGS GO WRONG

I TRY MY BEST TO BE SELF-AWARE. I think it's a very important skill that helps relationships become healthier. But it's not easy. I'm working on it.

For example, when people come to Milestone for the first time, I realize many of them will look at me when they're thinking to themselves, *What are these people all about?*

I'm not crazy about this idea, because there's so much more to our spiritual family than me, but I get it. I do the same thing when I go to any place and I'm trying to get a sense of what they're all about.

If you're thinking, *Okay, Jeff, you're really into this church deal. But let's be honest: you have to be. If you're like the rest of us, you'd probably realize church doesn't always work this way.*

Believe me. I understand. I'm very familiar with the frustrations and limitations people carry in their minds when they think about church. But even though I'm aware, I have not given up on the idea of what church can be.

Not because I have these great plans for it, but because Jesus does.

Let's go back to the story Jesus told in Matthew 13:44 to compare His Kingdom to a man who finds the treasure buried in the field. Most people only saw a field of dirt, but once this man found the treasure, he went in his joy and willingly sold everything he had so he could buy the dirt because he saw the value.

Unfortunately, the majority of people who look at church see more dirt than treasure.

There are several reasons why this happens.

① We form our opinions of church based on our experiences.

This is normal. It's how life works. But we have to be open to the possibility there may be more out there than the version of church we experienced.

Or maybe you've never had any experience with church at all. I've found people in this group think this somehow disqualifies them or puts them in a lesser category. Not to me! There is nothing I get more excited about than meeting someone, especially later in life, who comes to church for the very first time. It's an honor and a privilege. I take it as an incredible gesture of trust.

② We have an enemy.

He is committed to tearing down and criticizing our view of God's plan and accusing and undermining the Church at every opportunity.

③ We encounter relational challenges in church.

There is no perfect church, because every church is filled with imperfect people. All of us will get offended. We'll go through storms and challenges and have to deal with hurt.

How we respond to these challenges will be determined by how we view the Church and whether or not we share God's vision for the value and worth of His Church.

This is not theory to me—I have had to make this choice over and over in all kinds of different circumstances.

Defining Moments

I grew up going to church with my family every Sunday. I never struggled to believe in God and I didn't mind going to church. But after a while, I started to wonder what the point was.

THERE IS NO PERFECT CHURCH, BECAUSE EVERY CHURCH IS FILLED WITH IMPERFECT PEOPLE.

I knew the kinds of behavior we were *against,* but I couldn't tell you our clear, intentional goal. And perhaps most troubling of all, I could not find the kind of people of influence or significance I hoped to one day become.

But then I had one of those defining moments.

I distinctly remember hearing the gospel message at twelve years old—it captured my heart and my imagination. It still does all these years later. I remember giving my life to Jesus around my family's kitchen table. I wanted Him to be the Lord of my life, and I promised to serve Him forever. I was baptized a week later.

But as I sat in my room a few months later, I heard a clear, distinct message: "I am calling you to ministry." The impression was unmistakable, and I immediately knew without a doubt that it was God who was calling me.

My twelve-year-old brain could barely grasp what my plan was for the rest of the summer, much less the rest of my life. I knew I hadn't called myself—God had called me. I figured if He wanted me to do it, He'd provide a way to make it happen. And He did.

My mom is a prayer warrior, so when she heard this news she said, "Thank you, Jesus! I knew it." My dad was an engineer, so his response was more measured. He reached in his pocket protector, pulled out a pen, and said, "Sit down, boy. We're going to figure out how you're going to pay your bills."

God helped me every step along the way. My pastor invited me into his home often and taught me how to lead and serve people. By the time I was sixteen, he was letting me preach. When I left home to go to college at Baylor University, my goal was to become the most dynamic and effective ministry leader I could be.

The leaders and relationships I met at "Jerusalem on the Brazos" (one of my favorite nicknames for Baylor) added passion and excitement for my future. Once again, God was laying out the plan for my next steps and the calling He invited me to follow.

I went to college to get trained and to begin my career—not to find a wife. So you can imagine how surprised I was when God supernaturally orchestrated a situation to cross my path with a beautiful young lady named Brandy.

Our moms knew each other; they'd spent a season walking and praying together in the mornings. Let me tell you, something miraculous happens when a mom prays. The Bible says that when two or more come together and agree about anything, they'll receive it.[1] And if those two are moms? Forget it.

I may be a little slow to catch on, but I'm not stupid. Before long, Brandy and I were engaged to be married.

The pressure of finishing school, an impending wedding, and all the responsibility of taking care of my new bride accelerated my need for a clear plan beyond school. At that time, I was doing all kinds of youth events—speaking at camps, youth rallies, and retreats—and I liked the freedom of not being tied down to one local church. My sense of adventure was at odds with the prospect of being stuck in a daily grind as a pastor with people who didn't really want to be led.

[1] Matthew 18:19-20

My mentor/ministry leader at Baylor was a former president of a large evangelical denomination. He believed so deeply in my calling and my gifts and talents that he wrote my parents a letter describing in detail the future he believed God was preparing for me. He wanted me to put my name into the school's ministry guidance and placement center, where churches with job openings searched to find candidates that they were interested in.

You know how when you look back on your life you realize later when you come to one of those fork-in-the-road moments? They don't always feel like a big deal at the time, but they actually alter the trajectory of your life. Some people call them "sliding doors."

This was one of those.

Two job leads came back to me. The first was leading the youth program at a large, established church with a decent salary and a nice expense budget. The second was a youth director position at an older, smaller church in need of a lot of help—all for the lucrative salary of $50 a week.

I wanted door #1, but God was clearly leading me to door #2. Somehow I managed to obey. I took the tougher job at the smaller church for less money.

The "Temporary Interim" Pastor

I was the youth director at this small church where the average age put the "senior" in citizen, if you know what I'm saying. This was more than a modest adjustment from my previous experience in youth ministry.

But I was filled with passion and excitement and grateful for the opportunity, so I did whatever they asked—including lead the "music team." What I lacked in technical ability or musical talent, I made up for in contagious enthusiasm.

After six months, the pastor came to me and told me that he didn't want to be there anymore. He told me he'd felt this way for a while—he wanted to go back to school and get a master's degree in history. He said he'd already talked to the deacons and they'd agreed to make me the "temporary interim" pastor.

I ignored the fact that this was the most tentative job title in the history of ministry—and maybe the most redundant. "Temporary" is fairly clear. It means "not for long." But just in case there was any doubt in the uncertainty of my position, they threw the "interim" in there too. As in, "we're stuck with you until we get the person we want."

All of a sudden, I was a senior pastor at age 21. But I didn't say I was a good one. I often thought to myself, *I'm not sure I would follow me.* Before long, I realized I wasn't the only one who felt this way.

I didn't have much, but I did have a passion for God's Word. So as I preached every Sunday morning, people's lives started to change. Services started growing as new people came and brought their friends, lives were being impacted, and people were meeting together in small groups.

The church was growing—both in numbers and in diversity. This wasn't the same old church crowd. There were people from both sides of the proverbial tracks—from different neighborhoods, different backgrounds, different ethnicities—all coming together, united in worship of the God who made each of them unique.

I thought it was awesome. So when the leadership of the church called me in for a meeting on a Sunday afternoon, I thought I was getting a raise or at least a more permanent title. Maybe they'd just tell me how much they loved and appreciated us and the hard work we were doing.

Not so much—they were leaning in a slightly different direction.

"We want you to resign."

They were not pleased the church had attracted the "wrong crowd." I thought the wrong crowd meant people who were resistant to God, who didn't want to see lives transformed, or who were unwilling to change or be inconvenienced so others could come to know and love Jesus.

They believed the wrong crowd was anyone not like them— even when it was their own children.

I wasn't willing to fight about rules or programs. But I was willing to fight for people. People who were far from God, people who were lost, people who thought the church didn't understand them or didn't care what they were going through—these people weren't the wrong crowd. In my Bible, these were the people Jesus went looking for. So I tried to go looking for them too.

A Messy Breakup

My church wasn't afraid to kick people out. A few decades earlier, they excommunicated a struggling young musician and his sister.

Something about him bothered them, so they sent him packing. He crossed the street and started playing at another church, less than a stone's throw away.

I can't say for sure but I always wondered if this experience inspired him to write a song you'll probably recognize: "On the Road Again."

Yep. My church booted out Willie Nelson. Now they had their sights set on me.

They'd shake their keys at me from the pews if they thought I'd been preaching too long. I saw every version of their best stink-eye and heard them muttering under their breaths and whispering to each other. Brandy would come home and cry, and I'd just try to laugh it off. I called my regional support from the denomination, and they told me that I should just be patient and when something new opened up, I'd be first in line to get the spot.

Promises like that can encourage you for a moment, but they don't help so much when people start showing up at the parsonage (a house attached to the church where the pastor lives) looking to pick a fight.

Our lives had become the nightmare of most seminary students and new pastors. But believe it or not, looking back, I know God was doing something in our hearts that would last a lifetime.

In the midst of all this drama, I went to a large ministry event for men that was touring the nation. It was a really big deal, and one of my friends from Baylor was the son of the famous football coach leading it, so I got to meet these great men of God who were speaking to a football stadium filled with Christian leaders.

They preached powerfully about how God desires unity in the body of Christ. Meanwhile, my train-wreck of a church was the least unified in the entire body of Christ. I knew I had to do something.

I had been studying in 1 Corinthians where Paul writes that it would be better if we didn't gather as a church if we have anything against each other.[2] I'd also been thinking a lot about how Jesus said that if we don't forgive, we'll be tormented.[3] So that next Sunday morning, I took those two passages and went to church ready to do whatever it took to make it right.

I didn't just preach that morning—I poured my heart out over those two passages. When I came to the end, I told the church I was sorry for the mistakes I'd made as the pastor, and I wanted to forgive and do whatever needed to be done in order to reconcile the situation.

Nothing happened. Total silence.

For what felt like forever, no one said anything; no one even moved. Then a lady got up and said she'd harbored some unforgiveness against some of the leaders who were making things hard on me. The chairman of the deacons immediately stood up, looked at her, and said in a cold, harsh tone, "Sit down, lady. We don't need your forgiveness."

---

[2] 1 Corinthians 11:17-22
[3] Matthew 18:21-35

In that moment, I felt God say, "Enough." I looked to the people whose hearts were good and who'd been saved in that church and I told them to go to another church in town I trusted.

And then I turned to the people who were running me out and said, "If you guys want this building back so badly, you can have it, but based on your perspective, I don't think you can call this a biblical 'church.'"

I went to church that morning fully expecting to reconcile. I believed things were going to work out. I wasn't planning what came out of my mouth next. I hadn't even talked about it with Brandy, but the following statement changed our lives forever.

"Effective immediately, I officially resign as pastor."

They gave me a standing ovation. That will do a lot for your self-esteem.

Later that day they killed my dog.

After the adrenaline wore off, I went back to clean my office and knelt down and cried. I was fully committed to that little church. I wasn't looking for a way out or a reason to quit. I wanted to see God do incredible things in the community—and He was. I never imagined it would end that way.

It was a messy breakup. By Tuesday of that week, I'd packed everything we owned (which wasn't much) and moved in with my in-laws.

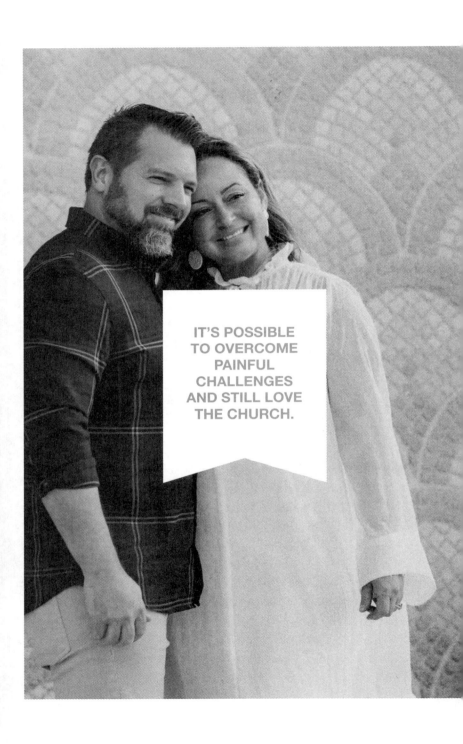

IT'S POSSIBLE
TO OVERCOME
PAINFUL
CHALLENGES
AND STILL LOVE
THE CHURCH.

You Can Still Love the Church

I did not share my story with you to make you feel bad for me. I told you so you could see how it's possible to overcome painful challenges and still love the church.

You might be thinking, *Seriously, Jeff? After everything you went through, that's what you're worried about? You're way too into this church thing!*

One of the things I hope you learn is how Jesus feels about His Church. In case you're wondering, He really loves it. It's the only thing He promised to build. Through Him, it's the hope of the world. It's His family, His body, His bride, His hands and feet in the earth.

This is why the enemy works so hard to distort, slander, resist, and vilify the Church at every turn. He knows that if he can cut you off from the Church, he can cut you off from God's plans, God's blessings, and the very relationships you need to find the help and healing you're looking for.

Does the Church need to grow and mature? Of course. Are there mean, hurtful hypocrites in church? Yes. But the longer I live, the more I realize you can find those people in every workplace, every classroom, every family, and every other place people gather.

But here's why this is so tragic:

- If a restaurant messes up your order, you don't stop eating food.
- If a teacher lies, you don't give up on learning.
- If a referee misses a call, you don't quit the sport.

- If an accountant cheats, you don't throw out your budget.
- If a doctor mistakenly diagnoses your sickness, you don't walk away from medicine or treatment.

And yet, when people have a bad experience with church, they give up on church. Sometimes they give up on God altogether.

All they see is dirt—and they miss the treasure in the field waiting to be discovered.

My prayer is that every person overcomes the challenges, hurts, and lies of the enemy to discover the beauty and the blessing God gives through being a contributing member of His Church.

This was our dream when we started Milestone Church, and we celebrate every time God does it again.

KEY THOUGHTS

- Jesus said you have to look past the dirt to find the treasure. Unfortunately, many people who look at the church see more dirt than treasure.

- There are three major challenges that keep us from seeing church the way Jesus does:
    1. Our past experiences with church
    2. The enemy
    3. Relational challenges and offense

- Having a bad experience with church is painful, but it does not mean there's no such thing as a healthy church.

- It's possible to have painful experiences with church and still love it and remain committed to Jesus' plan to build His Church.

NEXT STEPS

—If you've experienced one of the three major challenges (or all of them), have you worked through what you went through? Do you still believe that through Jesus, the local church is the hope of the world? What would it take for you to believe that?

3

WHAT DOES GOD THINK ABOUT CHURCH?

AS A PASTOR (AND A PARENT), I've learned people have opinions whether or not you invite discussion. I've found it's better to invite the conversation. You want people talking with you instead of talking around you. So let's talk about it.

What do you think of when you hear the word "church"?

- You might picture a quaint church building with a steeple or a cross.
- You might think of an ornate cathedral in a metropolitan center.
- Some people might think of a place you go for weddings, funerals, or to celebrate Christmas and Easter.
- Since you're reading this book, you may think about a weekly gathering filled with music and a message.

There is a reason you think this way. We form these opinions based on our experiences, what we've heard from friends or family, or even what we see in popular culture or media.

If church is an optional activity, only meaningful for some people, then it becomes like a movie or restaurant recommendation—potentially helpful but largely forgotten.

Or what if church is like eating kale, flossing, or going to the gym? We know it's good for us and it will improve the quality of our lives, but it can be difficult to find the motivation to consistently follow through.

When most of us consider trying something new, we usually ask ourselves some version of this question: *What am I going to get out of this?* This makes sense. I do the same thing.

When it comes to church, I think most people are interested in similar things. Maybe their priorities are different, but most people *want to become a better person* (to grow spiritually), they *want to make some friends*, and they *want help with their family or the relationships they care about the most.*

I get it. I value all of these things. And I think being a committed part of a local church gives you a great opportunity to experience meaningful help in each of these areas.

But I don't think it's the best place to start. If we really want to know why, we have to start with the person who designed it. What were they thinking? What did they have in mind?

Let's ask it this way: *What does God think? How does He feel about church?* We don't have to guess—all we need to do is consider what He said about it in His Word.

Jesus was the first person to use the word "church" in the Bible, in a very important story in Matthew 16. We'll go back to that story in a moment.

But when you look at Scripture as a whole, the most common illustrations used to communicate the concept of the church are God's people, His family, or His body.

How does God feel about His Church? Here are a few examples of what the Bible says:[1]

- Jesus promised to be with them, whenever they gathered together, and encouraged them to pray and ask anything in His name *(see Matthew 18)*.
- Jesus prioritized unity in the Church while focusing on reaching those outside the Church; He prayed for those who would come to know Him through the Church, and He said the whole world would believe in Him because of the way they loved each other *(see John 17)*.
- When the Church first started, they were in awe of what God was doing, they gathered in different places daily, and people were being saved every day *(see Acts 2)*.
- God said His wisdom would be made known through His Church *(see Ephesians 3)*.

---

[1] Matthew 18:19-20; John 17:21-26; Acts 2:42-46; Ephesians 3:10; 5:25-32; Hebrews 10:24-25.

- Jesus loves the Church the way a faithful husband loves his wife *(see Ephesians 5)*.
- The Church spurs each other on to love and good deeds when they meet together and encourage one another *(see Hebrews 10)*.

I Will Build My Church

Let's go back to the first time the word "church" shows up. In Matthew 16, Jesus takes His disciples to a place called Caesarea Philippi. This was a beautiful, lush region where the headwaters of the Jordan River flowed. There was a cave with a large hole in the ground where steam emerged, and the people believed this was a doorway to the spiritual world. This place had many names, including "The Gates of Hell."

The kings and rulers of the area all knew this was a special piece of property. There was an annual pagan festival that attracted large crowds and included extreme sexual and violent worship practices. You can understand why any devout Jew would avoid this area, but this is where Jesus decided to introduce His vision for His Church.

He brings the disciples to this intimidating, terrifying spot and asks them who the people say He is. Then He asks them the same question. In one of his moments of brilliance, Peter gives the perfect answer. He responds by saying, "You are the Messiah, the Son of the living God."

Peter was saying, "You're God's promised King. The One we have been waiting for from the very beginning. The One true and faithful Son who will make right everything that has gone wrong."

Jesus affirms Peter's answer and tells him that on this understanding—on the belief that Jesus is the King, the long-awaited Son of God who has come to save the world—He will build His Church. And "The Gates of Hell" (the darkest, scariest, most evil thing they could think of) would not be able to overcome this Church.

*The word "church" means "called out ones."
It's people. It's always been about people.*

I've been to this place in Israel a few times. This is one of the key passages in the history of our church. And when I think about these words, thousands of years later, the most amazing part of this passage is Jesus' promise: To build. His. Church.

You may have never thought of it this way, but it's the only thing He ever promised to build.

Jesus had options. He could have built all kinds of things. Vocal segments of the Jewish people wanted Him to be a political ruler and overthrow the Romans. He refused.

He only had one plan—His Church—and He has not given up on His plan. His family. His body. His bride. This is how Jesus feels about His Church.

The Bible shows us a picture of what this Church will eventually look like in Revelation 7:9—a great multitude no one could count, made up of people from every nation, tribe, people, and language. What an incredible picture.

This is what Jesus thinks about when He thinks about His Church—people of every ethnicity, from every part of the planet, with all kinds of different experiences and backgrounds, gathered together in the unity that only comes from a genuine relationship with Him.

JESUS HAS NOT BROKEN HIS PROMISE TO BUILD HIS CHURCH.

When this family comes together in genuine unity and offers their gifts out of their love for Jesus and their desire to contribute their part to His mission, nothing can stop them.

It's *that* Church that has moved the cause of Christ, God's mission of redeeming the world, through human history. Jesus' Church has toppled empires; stopped slavery and oppression; built schools, orphanages, and hospitals; fed the hungry; healed the sick; cared for widows and prisoners; loved the lost; preached the good news; ministered through God's Spirit; and stood strong as the enduring pillar of the community.

Obviously, not every local church does all those things, but every great local church preaches the gospel, makes disciples, inspires the hopeless, comforts the hurting, challenges the proud, and passionately loves and serves its community.

Though you may have never heard of them, there are tens of thousands of these kinds of churches all over the world. God has not given up on the Church that His Son died for. And Jesus has not broken His promise to build His Church.

Jesus is a wise master builder. We love and value both the "C" Church (the body of Christ throughout the earth) and the "c" church (the local church gathered in Jesus' name). Every church has its own stewardship, its own distinctives, and its own values and strategies. Not every church is called to reach the same people using the same methods. There is room for a variety of expressions while remaining faithful to the authority of God's Word.

And one of the primary commandments is for the people of God to love and honor one another.[2]

We are humbled by what God has done through Milestone Church and we understand we are one small part of the greater whole. We are an expression of God's heart—there are lots of ways to do church, and we love and stand with all of our brothers and sisters in Christ building God's Kingdom throughout the earth.

---

[2] Matthew 22:36-39: "'Teacher, which is the greatest commandment in the Law?' Jesus replied: "'Love the Lord your God with all your heart and with all your soul and with all your mind.' This is the first and greatest commandment. And the second is like it: "Love your neighbor as yourself.""

When we really understand God's plan for His Church, it's stunning. It's beautiful. It's so much bigger than what we think. And when you see it in action, it's miraculous.

The Church Keeps Moving Forward

You may think I'm naive, biased, uninformed, or just plain wrong, but I genuinely believe that *through Jesus, the local church is the hope of the world.*

No one would argue that at times the church has failed miserably, lost its way, forgotten its story, and lost its identity because of human sinfulness. The problem was not the plan; it was the inability to live up to what God designed.

But think about this: despite these grievous leadership mistakes, constant opposition, unimaginable persecution, and insurmountable challenges, not only has the Church endured, but it continues to grow on a daily basis and expand around the globe.

Global political empires rise and fall. Fortune 500 companies come and go. And yet, despite all its challenges, the Church keeps moving forward. It has been expanding for more than 2,000 years.

The only reasonable way to explain this is because God chose the Church to be His people—to be the extension of His blessing and His primary instrument for ministry in the earth.

As the body of Christ in the earth, the Church provides genuine comfort for hurting hearts. It teaches compassion, generosity, spiritual family, and serving to meet practical needs and move forward into a new tomorrow. It offers a way out of the prisons

ONLY THE
GOSPEL
OF JESUS
EXPRESSED
THROUGH
BOTH WORD
AND DEED CAN
TRANSFORM
THE HUMAN
HEART.

of bitterness, anger, and vengeance through the miracle of forgiveness. And only the gospel of Jesus expressed through both word and deed can transform the human heart.

The government can't offer this hope—neither can Wall Street or Fortune 500 companies.

When it's healthy, the local church is the most resource-rich environment on the planet. The Church has the largest participation, the widest distribution, the longest continuation, the fastest expansion, the highest motivation, the strongest authorization, the simplest administration, and the key role in God's conclusion of history.

That's why, even in a nation that treasures the separation of church and state, even among reports of decreased confidence in organized religion and the rise of the number of Americans with no religious affiliation, the Church keeps moving forward.

Though it is often maligned and overlooked, there is nothing else like it on the planet. Through Jesus, the local church is the hope of the world.

The Greatest Cause on Planet Earth

God designed the Church to carry out His mission and to bring His Kingdom to the earth. Paul described it this way in Ephesians 3:10: ". . . so that the manifold wisdom of God might now be made known through the church to the rulers and authorities in the heavenly places . . ."[3]

----

[3] NASB

The Church is not about a building, and it's not about people holding on and hiding out, trying desperately to protect an old-fashioned way of life. *The Church is God's only plan* to reverse the darkness we see everywhere around us in our culture.

I want you to look at this word Paul uses here: "manifold." This word means "multifaceted"—like a rainbow. Not the ROY G BIV you learned in kindergarten with seven basic colors, but the amazing optical miracle you see when light passes through water.

There are an infinite number of colors in the spectrum. As complex as the human eye is, you can't come close to picking out and identifying all of them. Paul is saying that God's wisdom, His love, His person, is so beautiful that you can't even begin to see it all. But the way He shows it to you is through His Church. When the Church lives the way God designed it to function, God's power is demonstrated to all His enemies.

> **Through Jesus, the local church is the hope of the world.**

A guest can't see this present yet invisible God...until they see Him working through the lives of His people. That's His Church—His hands and feet demonstrating His love in the lives of real people.

This isn't my idea; it's God's.

He doesn't think His Church is insignificant. He doesn't think it's a crutch for weak-willed, codependent people. The stakes aren't just life and death—they're bigger than that. They're eternal.

Don't ever underestimate the significance of what takes place when God's people come together and live as His Church. Every time you give, serve, love someone who's hurting, pray for the sick, invest time in the next generation, forgive, worship, connect to others relationally, it's not a small thing. You're not participating in irrelevant spiritual activities; you're joining God in His eternal purposes.

> God's mission on planet Earth has been entrusted to the Church.

When the Church becomes the Church that God created it to be, it declares to every ruler and authority in the earth that there is a higher Kingdom, a greater King, and a Prince of Peace who is on the move to redeem and restore the whole world.

These rulers and authorities are not people from a different political party or religious background. They are not the people we disagree with on social media. And they are not make-believe symbols of darkness to scare us into obeying God or becoming more self-righteous.

They are demonic spirits who have been around since the creation of the earth and they have been terrorizing and intimidating people as long as human beings have walked on this planet. They are a very real army, completely devoted to the torment and destruction of the things of God—which always ends with the prolonged suffering of people. This is their intended outcome in every age, in every culture, and in every place on the planet.

But they're no match for King Jesus and His Church.

So if this is what God thinks about "church," why don't more people experience it?

Keep reading and we'll find out.

KEY THOUGHTS

- The only thing Jesus ever promised to build was His Church.

- The Church has always been about people.

- The Bible calls the Church Jesus' body, His family, and His bride. In other words, He *really* loves it.

- Even with all the challenges, persecution, and obstacles, the Church has endured for more than 2,000 years.

- When it's healthy, the local church is the most resource-rich environment on the planet.

- Through Jesus, the local church is the hope of the world because the greatest cause on the planet has been entrusted to the Church.

NEXT STEPS

—Has your concept of the word "church" changed?

—Do you share the same high view that God has of His Church?

WHY IS IT CALLED MILESTONE CHURCH?

THERE ARE SO MANY WAYS TO DO CHURCH.

You can lead a church with big impersonal events, where large numbers of people come and watch the services. There are churches doing this well. The services are engaging, highly produced, and driven by content. The primary way people participate is by watching a few talented people use their gifts from the platform.

You can be a traditional church governed by strong denominational ties and run services through liturgy and the sacraments. The primary way people participate is through their affiliation or identification with the faith tradition.

You can be program-driven, where the church offers a wide range of preaching, classes, and Sunday school options. The primary way people participate is through learning and growing through age-appropriate classroom environments, retreats, conferences, study groups, and off-site gatherings.

You can gather around causes, issues, and politics, where the church is known for their commitment to meeting societal needs.

I am not suggesting you can find one on every corner or we've come anywhere close to the point where we should slow down planting churches, but if you're looking for any of these expressions of church, they're not hard to find.

They are prominent throughout North America, and you can find most of them in most places around the world.

And if they're preaching the gospel and advancing the Kingdom, we're for them. Every church has its own values, ethos, unique distinctives, and culture. If they're being who God's called them to be in a way that's biblical, we celebrate with them. We're not supposed to all be the same. There are different parts to the body of Christ and we're honored to be part of the family.

At Milestone, we have chosen to lead the church like a family. I'm not saying this is my idea—remember, this is how God describes His Church. We believe a church is more than a crowd of people gathered together to listen to spiritual content. It's more than a club you join after carefully weighing all the options. It's more than another membership card you add to your wallet.

We believe the Bible paints the picture of God placing people in the church the way people are added to a family. It's more than watching a message on your phone or listening to worship music in your car.

You attend. You serve. You give. You intentionally build relationships. You prioritize getting your family to church. You love and support the people God has put in your lives. You pray for your pastors and leaders. You value what Jesus values.

Your "church life" is not something you put on a couple times a month for an hour or two. It also does not mean you live your whole life at the church.

Instead, the relationships God places you in at church weave into your everyday life and impact how you think, how you grow into a better version of who God created you to be, how you navigate life's challenges, and how you celebrate life's greatest victories.

Why "Milestone"?

The word "milestone" is an old English term that dates back to the 1740s. A milestone was a stone that functioned as a milepost marking the distance in miles from a given point. Practically speaking, a milestone defined how far someone had gone in their journey and indicated how far they still had to go.

In several passages of the Old Testament, God tells people who are following Him

WE BELIEVE THE BIBLE PAINTS THE PICTURE OF GOD PLACING PEOPLE IN THE CHURCH THE WAY PEOPLE ARE ADDED TO A FAMILY.

to mark their journey with large stones as a memorial to what He was doing in their lives for all to consider. This happened during some of the most important moments in the journey of God's people.

They did this when they built altars out of stone. Sometimes they did it when they crossed over a river. These stones were markers reminding them of the faithfulness of God. One of the names given to Jesus is the great cornerstone.

When you would build a large structure in the ancient world, the foundation and the stability were anchored to the first stone you placed that held the whole structure together—the cornerstone.

All these thoughts about stone stuck with me as we prayerfully considered our name.

Though our circumstances may be different, I think many of us can relate. Maybe we've had moments with God that we marked—only to forget them later as life moved on.

But when you're on a team, when you're in a family, when you're walking in relationships where everyone's future hinges on your willingness to follow through, everything changes. When someone you care about is counting on you, you are willing to go the extra mile.

And then together, you celebrate. You mark the moment. You remember.

For too many people, church is a responsibility or a chore—a place where you go and make small talk and use words and phrases that you never speak anywhere else. You can't remember what happened there last week, much less last year.

We believe that's not how God intended it. We believe that each of our relationships with God should be marked by change—transformation. God is taking us somewhere. As we serve Him and walk through life together, our lives will be marked, just like these giant stones, by His undeniable presence and power at work in our lives.

When this happens, it's not just a big deal for us. It doesn't just make a difference in *our* lives. Our children will ask us, "What did God do in your life back then?" And when we tell them, it will mark their stories and our own. God's plan for your life is so much bigger than you. It should mark every significant relationship in your life—even the ones you don't have yet.

Released to Your Inheritance

Joshua is one of the great characters in the Bible, and his story comes to a close in Joshua 24. No other passage of Scripture had a greater impact on the name of our church. In this little story, I heard God communicate the kind of place He wanted Milestone Church to become.

The generation that God rescued from Egypt wandered and complained with Moses in the wilderness for 40 years, but in their place emerged a new generation. They believed God would go before them, they followed Joshua, and supernaturally, the Lord drove out all their enemies from the Promised Land. The majority of the second half of the book of Joshua is devoted to dividing the inheritance in this new land for God's people. Joshua challenges them to remember what God had done for them and to be faithful to live according to His Word.

GOD'S PLAN
FOR YOUR
LIFE IS SO MUCH
BIGGER
THAN YOU.

By the time we get to Joshua 24, Joshua is old and well advanced in years—he's giving his final appeal and blessing. He gathers all the people of God together and he reminds them of their story—the hundreds of years, the ups and downs, the incredible faithfulness of God that had brought them to this moment.[1]

He challenges all the people to fear the Lord, to serve Him with sincerity and in faithfulness by putting away the gods their fathers served before they crossed the river. He gives a famous command: "Choose for yourselves this day whom you will serve . . . but as for me and my household, we will serve the Lord."[2]

The people immediately respond: they want to serve the Lord. Joshua places a large stone in that place as a reminder to all the people of the promise they made together to serve the Lord and honor Him together.

"Then Joshua dismissed the people, each to their own inheritance."[3] This little sentence practically jumped off the page of my Bible.

The inheritance—the piece of land and resources that God was giving them—had been set aside long before this. But Joshua didn't release any of them until all of them had come together as a people. The shared commitment to what God had done in them, through them, and for them preceded them receiving what God had promised.

It may seem like a small detail, but the significance of this is huge. This is a markedly different attitude from the previous generation

[1] Joshua 24:1-13
[2] Joshua 24:15
[3] Joshua 24:28

Moses led out of Egypt. That group complained about everything. Like many of us, that group viewed the world through a simple filter: "What's in it for me?"

This new generation was more concerned with what God was doing through them for the sake of others. They didn't want what God was giving to them until they knew the rest of their family were provided for.

These two attitudes—these two ways of relating to God and evaluating life—still exist today. A Moses generation wants to know when they're going to get what they've been promised. A Joshua generation gives of themselves, out of their love for God, to see others receive the promises and blessings of God. And as a result, they're blessed in the process.

> A Joshua generation goes together. Their focus is not on themselves but on the people they're serving.

A Moses generation relies on the faith and obedience of their leader—when he succeeds, they succeed. They can't go to God on their own; he goes for them. He hears the voice of the Lord and relays it to them. When he fails or asks them to do something, they complain and go worship their own idols.

A Joshua generation goes together. Their focus is not on themselves but on the people they're serving. Receiving the promises of God was not something an individual did on their own; it was a process the entire group walked in together, like when all the people marched around Jericho or when all the people suffered because of the disobedience of Achan.[4]

I believe this principle hasn't changed. We're trying our best to build it into the fabric of Milestone Church.

We can be like the Joshua generation that believed God always blesses us to be a blessing.

It wasn't about creating their best and most fulfilled lives to bring them glory. It was about serving God's purpose in their generation and impacting those who would come after them. The reality is, there isn't a more fulfilling, significant way to live life.

The incredible paradox is that when you stop making your life about you and what you get, then, and only then, can you begin to experience the life you've been looking for all along.

The only thing better than being released into your own inheritance is to help someone else receive theirs.

We like to say, "We're an everyone church." Church is so much more than a few talented people on a platform. It's more than a building. It's the power of what happens when God makes a group of people a family. We don't all have the same gifts and talents. None of us can do everything, but all of us can do something.

We believe God has a place for every person to use their gifts, serve others, and grow into the best version of who God created them to be.

We've seen this at every step along the way.

---

[4] You'll find both of these fascinating stories in Joshua 6 and 7.

Reaching People and Building Lives

My first church experience was about as bad as it gets. I was ready to do something else. After leaving the church where they killed my dog, my wife and I moved in with her parents. She cried every day. As you can imagine, this was not ideal.

While I was frustrated, I had a strong sense God was not done with us yet. Before long, a new opportunity came to lead a church in the bustling metropolis of Chico, Texas. Brandy and I felt like God was opening this door, and so we went and saw Him do incredible things during that season. Some of the people we met there are part of Milestone today.

Through a series of relationships, God moved us from Chico to Abilene. Again, we were amazed by what God did in the lives of people, and we were honored to add to what the leaders who came before us had established. But we could not shake the sense that we were called to plant a church. We prayed and asked our pastors and trusted voices about several opportunities before settling on planting a church in Keller, Texas. Thirty-two people sold their homes and moved with us from Abilene to help us launch Milestone Church in the fall of 2002.

Our vision has always been, "Reaching people and building lives." You reach people who are far from God with the life-changing message of Jesus. And you build the lives of the people who have a relationship with God to become everything He created them to be.

You don't have to sacrifice one for the other.

The Cafetorium

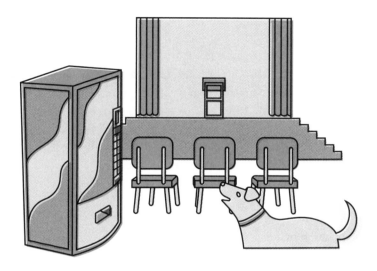

We started meeting at a middle school cafetorium—if you're not familiar, that's the room where the kids eat lunch and have assemblies. This means that while I was preaching, you could go over to one of the Coke machines, put in your dollar, and grab a soda. And people did.

Not everyone can keep their composure when a guest pops open a Coke while you're trying to feel significant and build a church, but God helped us. People who had never been to church gave their hearts and lives to Jesus. God was supernaturally adding people to our church who saw the vision of what we were trying to do.

Jim and Jeanne

Jim and Jeanne had been in many successful ministry environments. Jeanne is a very talented vocalist who led worship in stadiums across the country for years and yet she sensed God was calling them to be part of what God was doing at Milestone. Jim helped lead an international ministry with missions projects around the world and he offered to serve this church plant and has since served on our board for years.

Eventually, we outgrew our space and moved across Keller to a leased church building on Willis Lane. Our team loved the fact that we had a dedicated space and we didn't have to set up early every morning at the school; but before long, we were out of space again. These were not church people switching spots for upgraded services.

Eddie and Ginger

They were families like Eddie and Ginger, whose son (Eddie Jr.) was one of the first people God brought to Milestone. Eddie Sr. had multiple DUIs, his marriage was in trouble, and their family was hurting. But the love of God changed him, restored their marriage, and now Eddie and Ginger serve every weekend alongside their kids and grandkids and the hundreds of people they've invited to Milestone over the years.

Within a few years, we bought our own building on Keller Parkway behind Taco Casa (the house of the taco). It was a converted grocery store and it felt huge when we moved in. Yet once again, God brought all kinds of people as He continued to make good on His promise to build His Church.

Samera

Samera was a young lady who grew up in a Muslim family who gave her life to Jesus. She and her fiancé were looking for a church when she ran into Ginger at a coffee shop. They started coming and began to experience the power of spiritual family. Samera had been praying and trusting God to bring her parents into the kind of relationship with Jesus she had. Eventually her mom and dad visited, they gave their lives to Christ, and now they serve on the greeting team, welcoming others to our church family.

We had never experienced parking and space issues like we did behind Taco Casa. We used shuttle buses for staff and volunteers to maximize as many spots as we could and it still wasn't close to enough. God told me to look for 50 acres in Keller, and every real estate agent around told me it didn't exist. But God delivered on what He'd promised and we were able to secure the land.

The people of Milestone gave generously and we opened our Keller campus on Mount Gilead in the spring of 2017. As He has done at every step along the way, God has continued to reach people and build lives.

One of the things I know about the people in our area is that they want the people they love to share in the things they enjoy. They want to bring their friends, neighbors, and co-workers. They love to put signs in their yard to invite people to big weekends, like Christmas or Easter.

Bella

When she was nine years old, Bella was in the car when she noticed one of those signs inviting her to Milestone. She asked her grandpa if he would take her to church. He said yes, and when Bella came, she gave her life to Jesus in Milestone Kids and was baptized a few weeks later. Now her whole family comes to Milestone and is growing in their relationship with God.

This is the power of an everyone church. It's a family. It's not an organization; it's a place to call home. It's a place to find encouragement in life's greatest challenges, and the place to celebrate life's greatest moments.

We've gone on to open new campuses, to purchase additional property, to train new leaders, and to develop the next generation, as we continue to become a multi-ethnic, multi-generational, multi-campus church family. We've seen hundreds of people give their lives to Christ. And we're just getting started!

We recognize and remember these moments when God moves in our lives. We celebrate the milestones together with the family God has placed us in.

KEY THOUGHTS

- There are lots of different ways to do church. What churches value and the way they build determine the kind of experience people have.

- At Milestone, we have chosen to lead the church like a family. The Bible paints the picture of God placing people in the church the way people are added to a family.

- Joshua took a large stone and placed it among the people as a reminder of God's faithfulness. He told the people, "As for me and my house, we will serve the Lord."

- Our vision is "reaching people and building lives."

- We're an "everyone church." We believe God has a place for every person to use their gifts, serve others, and grow into the best version of who God created them to be.

NEXT STEPS

—Have you taken steps toward being part of this "everyone church"? The Growth Track is the best place to start. You can find out more at milestonechurch.com/growthtrack.

5

WHY DO WE NEED CLEAR VALUES?

EVERY CHURCH, EVERY LOCAL BODY of believers, has priorities—principles, causes, and issues that they believe are more important than anything else. We call these values.

Values shape culture. They inform decisions, guide strategy, create the grid for discipline and conflict management, attract certain types of people, and repel others. This is true in any environment—a business, a school, a family, and certainly a church.

Values are one of the most important ingredients in any church, because what a church values, it will become.

The truth is, a church will *only* become what it values.

Values aren't what you put on your website, cool phrases you paint on your walls, or what you frame in decorative artwork. Values are what you are investing your resources in—your time, your people, your creative energy, and your finances.

The reality is, many times, organizations have well-crafted, inspiring values on all of their materials and publications, but there's a significant gap between who they think they are and what they're modeling.

Unfortunately, in these cases, the organization and its leaders are caught in the uncomfortable and awkward position of seeing themselves differently from the way everyone else views them. Often they're the last to know. And many times, they're unwilling to believe what is painfully obvious to everyone else.

Do you remember the first time you heard your voice played back on a recording? Most people are caught off guard and respond in shock—"No way! I don't sound like that—do I?!" You don't see the gap until it becomes so clear you can't deny it. That's what this feels like.

Two Sets of Values

This difference between the values an organization hopes they have and the values they're actually modeling is common; they represent two sets of values—*aspirational* and *actual*.

Aspirational values are the values an organization hopes they have, the ones they put on their website and communicate in their promotional materials. They're the best-case scenario. They're the ones they talk about when they're trying to inspire their members.

The problem is, when you're actually interacting with the organization, you don't see the aspirational values. This is the culture they're aspiring to, not the values they're living with every day.

They're idealistic, but they're not realistic.

Every retail business will tell you they value customer service, but the customer won't know for certain until they have a problem. You will soon discover whether the business is more interested in increased profits or your satisfaction.

Every school will tell you they value education, but students and parents may be surprised to discover their highest priorities are standardized test scores that lead to increased funding.

And nearly every church will tell you on their website that they value the Bible and serving people, but you won't find out until you enter the environment and realize what they celebrate.

> You can paint slogans on the walls and write compelling text on your website, but what you celebrate gets repeated.

Every environment has a culture that is built over time. Culture is what people feel when they interact with your organization. Cultures aren't developed through random events, one-time accidents, or unique circumstances. Culture is not random or arbitrary.

Culture is the result of intentional language, behavioral patterns, and expressed values modeled by leadership and implemented at every level of the organization.

When a visitor interacts with any department of your organization, their experience reveals what you value. Your environments, your deliverables, your language, and your priorities all communicate

WE NEVER OUTGROW THE NEED TO REFOCUS AND CLARIFY OUR VALUES.

your values. Put whatever you want on your website or on your walls, but once we interact with you, we'll discover what you really value.

Your values are so deeply embedded in your culture that they go far beyond the behavior of your staff and your volunteers. One of the comments we get repeatedly from visitors is how people go out of their way to welcome and include them. They expect the greeter or the guy in the parking lot to be nice and chat with them, but they don't expect it from the person sitting next to them in the sanctuary. That's another way you can spot the difference between actual and aspirational values.

As a pastor, I live with this reality on a daily basis. We never outgrow the need to refocus and clarify our values. It helps me to think of it this way: If I'm not sick of talking about our values, then our staff and our volunteers don't know them yet. And these are some of the most committed people in our environment.

You might be asking, "Jeff, why are you making such a big deal out of this?"

Great question. We're more focused and intentional about this than ever.

Here's why this is so important: Our world is filled with people who don't believe the church has anything to offer them. Or they've had a bad experience and given up on church—they don't think it works; they don't think that through Jesus it's the hope of the world. And one of the main reasons is that churches have been mismanaged or misled—nobody was asking these crucial questions.

Don't hear what I'm not saying. The church is not a business. It's not a company. We don't have customers. But God entrusts us with people, and one day I'm going to stand before Jesus and He's going to ask me what I did with the people He entrusted to me. I take this very seriously. I want to be able to say I did everything I could to create the healthiest environments possible.

Clear values answer the simple question "What are we trying to do?" Most people struggle to engage in environments where the answer is not obvious. It doesn't matter how large or successful a church appears to be. The moment this is no longer clear, the future is in trouble.

The importance of this clarity only becomes more vital as a church grows, because new people often bring new interests and emphasis. Without continuous clarity, the church eventually becomes distracted and ineffective as it is pulled in multiple directions at the same time.

Reaching People, Building Lives

I have already mentioned our vision, but it's worth repeating: reaching people and building lives.

Reaching people may sound nebulous and esoteric, but it's not to us. It couldn't be more clear. Reaching people means that men, women, and children are giving their lives to Christ—entering into a life-changing relationship with Jesus and committing to follow Him all of their days.

Building lives is equally measurable; it represents the personal growth of Christ-followers to serve and lead others. We believe it's our responsibility to do everything we can to develop every person into who God created them to be. The specifics of this are incredibly broad and diverse—moms, dads, students, businesspeople, pastors, entrepreneurs, grandparents, kids, doctors, lawyers, single moms, carpenters, small-business owners—but the values are shared.

Reaching people and building lives means you're continually thinking about messaging to more than one audience. How do you communicate to people who've never been to church in a way they understand while also connecting with and challenging committed followers of Christ?

While this requires a greater level of intentionality, it also reinforces the focus that although the church is a family consistently growing in love, it exists for those who have not yet come home.

Vision drifts and leaks toward the convenient and the comfortable. It's easy to forget. And if you're not careful, it doesn't take long to start talking in ways the average person struggles to follow.

AT EVERY POINT IN OUR JOURNEY, OUR FOCUS HAS BEEN AND WILL ALWAYS BE ON REACHING PEOPLE AND BUILDING LIVES.

At every point in our journey, our focus has been and will always be on reaching people and building lives. As we grow, we're constantly asking the question "Is what we're doing helping us to accomplish our vision?" If the answer is no, we stop doing it—no matter how long it's been a tradition or how much people enjoy it.

For example, from the earliest days of Milestone I would stand and shake hands with people after I preached. Like most church plants, we were trying to be as friendly and connective as possible in order to keep everyone coming. Over the years as the church continued to grow, at times I would consider, "Should I keep doing this?" I enjoy doing it. That wasn't the issue.

Was this communicating the right value? While it's not convenient or easy, I've realized it gives me the opportunity to model the authenticity, intentionality, and sincerity we value so much. We don't just *say* we value people; by doing this, I get a chance to actually show it.

And every weekend, someone comes up to me with a new idea, a new opportunity, a new program they are convinced Milestone should embrace. This isn't a bad thing; it encourages me to know people are filled with passion and ideas. In the early days I was tempted to accommodate everyone and do everything, but by God's grace we were able to keep our focus and continue to clarify values.

If we try to be everything to everyone, we create expectations we can't meet. It's not loving. It sets people up for hurt and disappointment.

We can't say yes to everything and maintain a clear, healthy culture.

Programs Versus Processes

Churches love programs. A program can be an event—like an annual men's retreat, a discipleship weekend, a leaders' gathering, a mission trip, a community service project—anything a church does to help accomplish its mission. A program can also become a ministry—for example, at Milestone we have a wide variety of ministry environments specifically designed for different demographics, circumstances, and seasons of life.

Programs allow you to specialize, to create subcultures, and to develop new leaders. But most programs have a shelf life. Programs are tools that exist to help you live out your values.

And once a program is no longer the best way to live out your values and accomplish your mission, you move on from it. Stale programs that have exceeded their expiration date are an energy drain on everybody. They kill momentum. They frustrate the people who lead them because they feel like nobody else cares about their program. They don't. Which is the other reason they're a drain—nobody wants to go, but often they care about the people leading it and they don't want to let them down.

We can't say yes to everything and maintain a clear, healthy culture.

Instead of programs, we need clear processes. A process is a clear, simple next step. It allows you to keep moving forward toward a common vision.

Simple next steps allow you to keep a bigger church feeling smaller.

When someone is considering coming to Milestone for the first time, we don't want them to feel overwhelmed. We want them to know we have plenty of space for them—to park their car, to check in their kids, and to find a great seat to enjoy their experience.

If they're like most of us, even before they visit, they'll probably take a look at our website or watch a service when they're making their decision. That's why it's important for them to find what they're looking for quickly. We want to help them plan their visit. We want them to feel like a welcomed guest.

And when they make it on campus, no matter how many people are walking and talking around them, we want them to feel like they know how to take their next step, make a friend, and feel included in what God is doing.

That's why we spend so much time and energy talking about our Growth Track. It's not a program where we're trying to give spiritual information to move people across the columns of a spreadsheet. Our team works really hard to personalize the experience to help them find what they're looking for—friends and a place to grow spiritually.

Discovery 101 helps them learn about the vision and values of Milestone, it connects them to people who are also taking steps, and it gives them the opportunity to meet our team so they feel personally connected to our church family.

Serve Team 201 gives them the opportunity to experience what it means to be an everyone church. They move from the stands to the playing field as they discover their gifts and unique contribution. In the process, they receive the fulfillment that comes from serving others while developing meaningful relationships with the other members of the team.

Values 301 is a seven-week journey where we dive deeper into our core values. Each week consists of a teaching by our pastoral staff to the large group, followed by a Small Group discussion. This is the ideal place for a first Small Group experience because the groups are formed based on similar seasons of life. We've found this gives people the greatest opportunity to make genuine friendships—the kinds of relationships that provide simple help for everyday errands, prayer and encouragement during challenges, and the people who celebrate life's great moments with you.

This is why we're constantly encouraging people to go through the Growth Track. We realize to you this sounds like, "Get involved in our church programs." We're not trying to add to your already busy calendar. That's not our goal.

We know you want to grow spiritually and find a place to belong, and we've discovered the Growth Track is the absolute best way we can give this to you.

How Do We Live This Out?

Our processes help us to ensure our values are actual and not aspirational. They're a big piece of the puzzle. And that's why we have to consistently evaluate our processes too. This requires a sense of trust and a willingness to be vulnerable.

As the lead pastor, this attitude has to begin with me. And it's not easy or comfortable. Our church is led by different groups of teams. I'm a member of these teams; I'm not the team. I like to say I don't really know how to do a lot of things, but I am good at finding really gifted people and inspiring them to work together.

One of the unique distinctions on many of our teams is the longevity of relationships. It's one thing to have talented people, which we do. But it's something different when these talented people work together over the span of 10, 15, 20+ years.

At the same time, these long-standing relationships don't prevent new members from joining. It creates trust and excitement that motivate the team to continue to expand.

This is how great teams work. On any great team you have to listen; you have to compromise; you have to put the goals and values of the team ahead of yourself; you have to know when to hold your ground and when to defer.

This requires a continued commitment to honesty, trust, and growth in your relationships. We have to invite feedback; we have to evaluate what and how we're doing; we have to be willing to have the difficult, critical conversations necessary in order to keep moving toward our goals and our vision.

The truth is, this is the kind of team everyone wants to be on. It's not easy but it is fulfilling and life-giving.

Living this way closes the gap between the aspirational and the actual, and it creates a culture of openness and trust, but I have to warn you: you may get a few bruises in your feelings along the way.

I live this way not because it's easy or comfortable but because I don't want there to be a gap between the me I think I am and the me everybody else lives with. I want my values to be actual— to be lived out in each of my relationships. That won't happen without constant evaluation.

Over the next few chapters, I'll describe our values in detail, why they're so important to who God has called us to be, and how we live them out on a daily basis in all our environments.

KEY THOUGHTS

- Values are important because what a church values, it will become. In fact, a church will only become what it values.

- Every organization has two sets of values— *aspirational* and *actual*. Aspirational values are who you hope to become. Actual values are who you really are.

- Clear values help you answer the simple question "What are we trying to do?"

- Programs are tools that help you live out your values; they should stop when they're no longer useful.

- Processes are clear, simple next steps that keep you moving toward a common vision.

NEXT STEPS

—Can you answer the question "What are we trying to do?" Could you explain it to someone else? What's the process that helps you answer this question?

SECTION 02

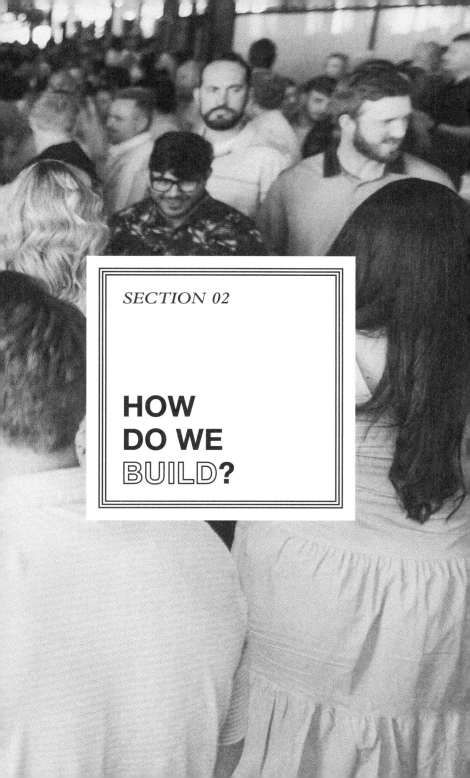

SECTION 02

HOW
DO WE
BUILD?

THE BIBLE
IS WORTH IT

OUR WORLD IS FILLED WITH NOISE.

All day, every day, we're surrounded by voices clamoring for our attention. Whatever dominates our attention fills our mind. Whatever fills our mind shapes our thoughts. Our thoughts shape our feelings, and our feelings dictate our behavior.

Something is going to have the loudest voice in our lives. And whatever has the loudest voice ends up with the greatest influence. This could be cultural narratives, the opinions of our friends and family, or our feelings.

I believe the best choice we can make is to set the Bible up as the highest voice—the ultimate standard of truth in our lives.

We value the Bible as God's revealed truth and the catalyst for lasting transformation and life change. The Word of God is one of the greatest gifts He has given us. It's so many things: divinely inspired, relevant, applicable, perfect, supernatural, simple, complex, comforting, and challenging.

It literally is the last word—nothing will be added to it, and it has the final say in the questions of how we live our lives, lead our families, and function as a church.

Because this is such an important concept, I wanted to think of a visual way to make it both real and memorable. At the very first Discovery 101, while I was talking about this, I took a Bible and held it over my head. It stuck with me, so I've done it in every 101 since then.

The idea is that everything else— opinions, cultural trends, thoughts and feelings—are all under the Word.

I don't value God's Word because I'm a pastor, because I'm supposed to, or because of tradition. I value God's Word because I desperately need it.

The Bible is the primary means by which we relate to God, grow closer to Him, and understand who He is, what He cares about, and how He's called us to live.

We can't live the life God's created us to live without a healthy and growing relationship with His Word.

What Is the Bible?

Not only is the Bible the best-selling book of all time, but the desire to replicate it was the driving force behind the invention of the printing press. Gutenberg invented his machine with the goal of creating his masterpiece—the Gutenberg Bible manufactured sometime in the 1450s (out of the 48 that still exist, one is currently displayed in the New York Public Library).

The word "Bible" literally means "the book." In other words, we have *any* books because we have *the* book. Without any exaggeration, the Bible is the most important book in the history of the world.

Practically speaking, the Bible is more than a book; it's a collection of books. It's more *library* than *book*. Over a span of nearly 1,500 years, forty men used three different languages to write the sixty-six different books included in the official canon (collection) of Scripture. God partnered with all kinds of people to write down His words—prophets, kings, shepherds, farmers, tax collectors, fishermen, doctors, and even a tent-making religious scholar.

And yet, the guiding principle throughout this library is not to inundate us with facts, characters, mysterious details, hidden conspiracies, or secret codes. This library tells one big story that points to one character—Jesus. The purpose of the Bible is to show us who God is through Jesus, *the living Word*. Whenever we get stuck while reading Scripture, we should ask the question, *how does this show us who Jesus is?*

Because of its prominence, the Bible has been criticized more than any other book, and yet its influence remains. The trustworthiness of Scripture has been ridiculed and attacked for centuries by some of mankind's most gifted thinkers. The problem is, the facts overwhelmingly favor the Bible.

THE PURPOSE OF THE BIBLE IS TO SHOW US WHO GOD IS THROUGH JESUS, THE LIVING WORD.

In the context of its culture, the Bible was miles beyond anything the world had ever seen in its dignity for servants, women and children, the poor, the sick, and even enemies. The origin of hospitals, universities, music and the arts, and the end of the European slave trade can all be traced back to the body of Christ in the earth. The writers of the Bible also included all kinds of embarrassing details about themselves that, let's be honest, I would have left out to make myself look good if I was telling the story.

The Bible has always challenged the prevailing opinions of any culture. It continues to challenge us today. No matter how popular opinion shifts around certain key issues, the authority of God's Word remains.

3 Examples of Biblical Authority

1. The Bible is clear in its condemnation of racism. Because it includes the story of broken humanity, there are racist attitudes, but in sharp contrast God always moves toward the margins to love and redeem those who've been placed on the outside.

2. Scripture dismisses the idea that there are multiple pathways to peace with God. Jesus made it clear: the road is narrow. There is no other way to the Father except through Him. While this may sound arrogant or unnecessarily exclusionary if it's misguided, if in fact it's true, then it's the most loving position the Bible could take.

3. The unwavering biblical standard for marriage is one man and one woman. This has become especially contentious as opinions have changed. The Bible hasn't changed. We see the same perspective from Genesis to the Gospels to the New Testament letters.

In Matthew 19:3-6, the Pharisees question Jesus about marriage. He responds by pointing them back to God's original plan in Genesis 2:24: "a man shall leave his father and mother and be joined to his wife . . . what God has joined together, no person is to separate."[1]

Paul affirms both Genesis and Jesus when he writes about marriage in Ephesians 5. This union is particularly important to God because marriage is more than a human relationship designed to bring love and happiness; it's a picture of the relationship between Jesus and His Church.

---

[1] NASB

In any of these examples, God does not force His will upon humanity. Human beings are free to come to different conclusions. But this freedom is not a license to reinvent God's truth or to change His standards or values into their own liking.

As for manipulating people by twisting Jesus' words, it turns out that lots of people wanted to make a name for themselves by writing their own version of a gospel—portions of more than 28 of them have been discovered. The early church dismissed them because they were fabricated, riddled with crazy thoughts, and not inspired by the Holy Spirit.

And what about the guys who actually wrote what we consider the New Testament? Nearly all of them were murdered because of what they believed. If they had fabricated or manipulated Jesus' words, they probably wouldn't have been willing to die to protect their secret.

Tens of thousands of ancient manuscripts of the Bible have been discovered and their consistency is remarkable. This demonstrates the authenticity of God's Word—these manuscripts don't just agree in concepts and big ideas; they line up in phrases, words, and, in most cases, each letter.

Why Did God Give Us the Bible?

Research shows that most people want to learn more about the Bible. Unfortunately, the same studies show that, for many people, that's as far as they get. It never moves from an aspirational value to an actual one.

Part of the problem is a misunderstanding of *why* we read the Bible. We're not studying for a test or memorizing facts for Bible trivia. Remember, it's a library that tells one story that points us to the person of Jesus—so that we might know and love Him more. That's why the Bible exists.

God's Word is the primary way He shows us who He is. This is the guiding principle for studying Scripture. Because of this, reading the Bible is how we learn to hear His voice—it's far more *relational* than *informational*.

So many things have changed over the multiple decades I've served people as a pastor. But what hasn't changed are the basic needs of the human heart. We all want to know God's will for our lives. We want to hear His voice. It's not as mysterious as we make it. If we meet Him in the Bible on a consistent basis, we won't miss it.

> **Reading the Bible is how we learn to hear God's voice.**

Whether you have five minutes or an hour, start your Bible reading time with a quick prayer in your own words. "Jesus, I've come to read Your Word because I want to know You more. Speak to me through Your Word. I'm ready to listen."

This is a prayer Jesus has already promised to answer. He told us in John 10:3 that His sheep hear His voice. He calls them by name and He leads them as their shepherd. If you're one of His sheep, this promise is for you. Remember, reading the Bible is more about a relationship than information.

What Keeps Us from Reading the Bible?

There are three primary reasons we don't read the Bible:

① "I don't know what this has to do with my life."

It's not always easy to connect the dots between an ancient text and our modern world. *What in the world does Leviticus have to do with how we live today? What do I do with the Old Testament? How do I apply this agricultural principle to my daily life? How do I take what Jesus said and apply it to my life in a meaningful way?*

I've watched some people get excited about reading their Bibles, and initially they're highly motivated. They can't wait to get started. And then it fizzles out. It wasn't their intention; they just didn't know how to make progress.

I've found no one enjoys doing something when they feel inadequate. This is why we don't do this alone. We get help.

With just a few simple steps I believe anyone can learn to benefit from time in the Bible on a daily basis. One of the most amazing things about God's Word is, it's simple enough for children to grasp but so deep even the brightest minds consistently discover new and incredible insights.

② "I don't have time."

We all get the same amount of time on a daily basis. The real issue is, what do we do with the time we've been given? Most of us *kill time* when we're delayed, *spend time* when we're learning/ working, and *make time* for the things we really care about.

When we're really passionate about something (our business, a hobby, sports, pop culture, etc.), no one has to tell us to get updates, search out new information, talk about it with other people who share this passion—we just do it.

We learn the Bible the same way we learn anything else—through time and attention. This brings up one of the most difficult challenges we have in our world today when it comes to managing our time.

No generation in history has had more distractions than we do. How many times each day are we distracted by the latest notification when we sit down to focus on something? Both our time and our attention can be stolen. Some of the smartest people in the world spend their lives thinking of ways to capture our attention because it is so valuable.

But when we understand how critical this time in the Bible is, we can be vigilant to protect it.

③ "Someone else can do it for me."
I love learning from other people. I love great preaching because it helps the Word come alive, and it causes me to know and love God more. Obviously, I believe we benefit from this type of growth. But it does not replace the need we all have to grow in our own relationship with God

WE LEARN THE BIBLE THE SAME WAY WE LEARN ANYTHING ELSE— THROUGH TIME AND ATTENTION.

through His Word. It's not enough for me to know the Word—
He wants *you* to know it.

Throughout Church history, whenever people drifted from the
Word and went to other people's thoughts or ideas, bad things
happened. The quickest way to get off track is to move away
from the Word, especially in big areas like the nature and character of God, how He offers salvation, and how He deals with sin.

I think this is an even bigger issue for us today because not only
is Bible literacy down, but also literacy and rational thinking in
general are down. We've changed the way we approach learning.
There's a big difference between knowing something and Googling
it. Web searches leave us at the mercy of someone else's perspective,
and as we all know, not everything on the internet is true.

> **The quickest way to get off track is to move away from God's Word.**

Think about this: For at least the first 1,900
years of the Christian faith, the average
follower of Christ did not have their own
copy of the Bible. That's not our problem.

We have Bible apps, audio Bibles, Student
Adventure Bibles, family Bibles, picture
Bibles—every kind of Bible you can
imagine. But being *around* the Bible is not
the same as being *in* the Bible.

The most extensive spiritual-growth study ever done showed
that the single greatest determining factor in the life of a believer
was consistent time spent in the Word. This is not something we
want to outsource. It is the foundation for spiritual growth and
Christian maturity.

How Do I Get Started?

I want to make this as practical as possible. This is not an exhaustive list, but if you do these things, I promise you will see dramatic improvement.

① Study the Word in church.

It's not easy and it requires effort, but this is where it starts. From the beginning, the people of God gathered to study the Word together. Jesus did this regularly. The modern idea of a "quiet time" with you and God being enough is not the biblical picture.

The first thing you need to do is commit to study the Word in church. Listen, pay attention, take notes, talk about it in Small Group, and reflect on it during the week. I can't overstate the importance of this.

In our weekend services and in all of our ministry environments, we always try our best to model a coherent, accessible approach to studying, interpreting, and applying Scripture. This is highly intentional. Our goal is to model what this looks like together so you will have the confidence and the ability to do it on your own.

You will learn how to do this on your own as you learn to do it with your church family.

② Make a daily commitment.

Start with a time frame you can consistently hit, even if it's just 5-10 minutes. As it becomes part of your daily routine, increase the number gradually. Picking the same time of day and location helps reinforce the habit.

If you can, use a physical Bible with a pen to underline or take notes in the margin instead of a device, to eliminate notifications and distractions.

③ Start in the Gospel of John.

I recommend John (the fourth book in the New Testament) because he clearly explains the significance of what Jesus is saying and doing. While the whole Bible points to Jesus, in John, He practically jumps off the page.

If you have the time, I also recommend reading one chapter from Psalms (how we relate to God) and one chapter from Proverbs (how we relate to each other) every day. Once you finish John, go back to the Gospel of Matthew and read through the rest of the New Testament in order.

If you've been reading the Bible for a while, there are all kinds of great reading plans available, and one of the best is reading the entire Bible in a year. Remember, it tells one big story that always points to Jesus.

④ Always read the Bible in context.

Most of the misunderstandings of Scripture happen when we take one tiny piece out and place it above everything else. We always want to read from the whole to the part. In other words, we need *all* of the Bible to understand *any* of the Bible.

Scripture is also filled with a wide variety of literary genres. The largest book is a song book (Psalms). We don't read song lyrics the same way we read a letter, poetry, historical narratives, wisdom sayings, or a list of commands.

While every part of God's Word has meaning *for* us, they weren't necessarily written *to* us. These stories happened in real time to real people. None of us start as a Bible scholar, but context leads us to ask all kinds of questions:

- Who wrote it and who were they writing to?
- What kind of literary genre is being used?
- How does it relate to what we know about the character of God from the rest of Scripture?
- How does it point to Jesus?
- How can it best be applied to us today?

A helpful tool in this process is often called the S.O.A.P. method. You start with a Scripture, you Observe what's happening, you Apply it to your life, and then you Pray and ask God to speak to you through the passage. This is a useful guide in developing your understanding.

⑤ Memorize and confess God's Word.

Once we memorize something, it's in us. Maybe you've noticed how your brain has this incredible capacity to retain trivia, song lyrics, and sports statistics. We want to be intentional about putting this power to work to get God's Word in us so we have it whenever we need it.

Psalm 119 is the longest chapter in the Bible. In verse 11, the author writes, "I have hidden your word in my heart that I might not sin against you." I love this picture. Why do we hide the Word in our hearts? Because our hearts need God's Word to live the life He wants us to live.

One of the best ways to memorize is to meditate. A biblical word picture for "meditate" is "to chew." I realize this may be a little gross, but I think it's helpful to think of how a cow constantly chews their cud because they have multiple stomachs. They chew for a while, it goes in their stomach, it comes back up—and they chew it again.

This is not the kind of meditation where you empty your mind; this is the kind where you fill it. Our minds will chew on something—whether it's our to-do list, worry, fear, anxiety, joy, or faith.

I'm always trying to get more of the Word in me. I place the Scriptures I'm meditating on in the high-visibility places in my life—the dash of my car, the back of my phone, even my bathroom mirror. When I see them, I memorize them; I meditate on them; I chew on them in my mind.

When we memorize something, it goes in. When we confess, it comes out.

As part of your daily reading, you should read and pray God's Word out loud. You get used to hearing the Word coming out of your mouth—it builds your faith, it causes your heart to align with God's Word, and it helps you know what to pray. It's so simple, but the impact is great.

What Happens When I Do This?

At this point you might be thinking, *Jeff, how do I know if it's working? What can I expect to happen?*

① Your thoughts and attitudes change.

Reading the Bible builds our character through challenging our mindsets and changing our perspectives. Hebrews 4:12 tells us that the Word is living and active, sharper than a double-edged sword, and it judges the thoughts and the attitudes of our hearts.

We don't just read the Bible; it reads us.

While the world tells us to follow our hearts, God's Word reminds us of the goodness of God and His promise to give us a new, clean heart that longs for the things of God instead of our selfish desires. Psalm 19 tells us that God's perfect laws are more precious than gold, they revive our souls, and they bring joy to our hearts.

② You develop a biblical worldview.

Every one of us has a worldview—our deepest, unchallenged assumptions about the world. Because the Bible has so much to say about how we live on a daily basis, consistent study of the Word helps us to align our hearts with God's perspective on how things work.

Our culture is filled with narratives—carefully crafted stories that attempt to explain why the world is the way it is. Many of these narratives are incredibly compelling; they appear to have definitive, concrete answers that help us make sense of the world. If we don't continually evaluate our worldview on the basis of God's Word, then we can easily be deceived by half-truths, faulty assumptions, and flat-out lies.

③ **Your faith grows.**

Romans 10:17 reminds us that the way we grow in faith is by hearing the Word of Christ. This is why it's important to read the Bible out loud, to pray God's Word, and to put it in places where we'll be reminded of it each day. Faith helps us to trust God's promises no matter what we're facing. We live by faith, not by sight.[2] It's through faith and patience that we receive the promises of God.[3]

When everything in the world starts to shake, the one thing you can count on is the Word of God. People anchor their lives to all kinds of things—their ability, their success, their favorable circumstances. But the only thing you can count on, the only thing you can be certain of, is the truth of God's Word.

[2] 2 Corinthians 5:7
[3] Hebrews 6:12

KEY THOUGHTS

- The Bible is the primary means by which we relate to God, grow closer to Him, and understand who He is, what He cares about, and how He's called us to live.

- The Bible tells one story and always points to Jesus.

- Reading God's Word is more relational than informational. We're not studying for a test; we're learning to know and love God more.

- What keeps us from reading the Bible?
    1. "I don't know what this has to do with my life."
    2. "I don't have time."
    3. "Someone else can do it for me."

- Practical ways to build the habit:
    1. Study the Word in church.
    2. Make a daily commitment.
    3. Start in the Gospel of John.
    4. Always read the Bible in context.
    5. Memorize and confess God's Word.

- We know we're growing in our understanding of the Bible when:
    1. Our thoughts and attitudes change.
    2. We develop a biblical worldview.
    3. We grow in faith.

NEXT STEPS ✓

—How would you describe the health of your relationship with God's Word? Write down a measurable goal for the next step in your growth.

—What is the biggest obstacle you face? Make a clear plan to overcome it.

—What is one of the practical steps you can take to grow in this area of your life? Commit to taking this step starting today.

7

THE MISSION IS WORTH IT

HERE IS A SIMPLE AND PROFOUND QUESTION:
What is God thinking about?

If you're like most people, you'd probably say, "I'm not sure, Jeff. How am I supposed to know?" I get it. It's a humble response.

And it shows you're not suffering from the Dunning-Kruger effect, which has become all too common. This is when people with limited to no expertise overestimate their knowledge.

But let's say we had to guess. What would you say? If you based your guess off what we see in Scripture, I would say the answer is clear: *people.*

God loves people. He cares about them. He is moved by their suffering. He longs for their healing and redemption. His heart consistently moves toward people—especially people who are far from Him.

From the Garden of Eden to the Red Sea, from the wilderness to the Promised Land, from Nazareth to Calvary, and throughout all of history, God has been at work to love, save, and restore people.

The Bible tells one big story that always points to Jesus. Why did the Father send His perfect Son to become a man, to live a perfect life, and to die a sinner's death? Why was He resurrected three days later? Why did He give the disciples the Holy Spirit and clear instructions to carry on His mission? What was the point?

What was His mission? Jesus makes it clear in Luke 19:10: "The Son of Man came to seek and save the lost."

Remember how we always read the Bible in context? In Luke 19, Jesus is passing through Jericho on the way to Jerusalem, where He will enter the city as God's long-promised King (we call it Palm Sunday), kicking off Holy Week, which will culminate with His betrayal and arrest, His death on the cross (Good Friday), and His resurrection (Easter Sunday).

There's a lot going on. It's a big deal. But right in the middle of all of this, Jesus sees a short tax collector named Zacchaeus. Tax collectors were the most despised people in their communities because they betrayed their own people for money. The people hated tax collectors—Jesus loved them.

He did not fail to see their sin, but He could see past it to the person created in the image of God who needed to be saved—just like the rest of us.

This little story takes place in Jericho, which was a historic military outpost on the edge of the Promised Land. God performed several miracles there to bring His people to the land He promised to give them, but He also cared about the people of Jericho. We know this because He worked through the life of Rahab, a prostitute living in Jericho, who the Bible honors as a woman of faith because she helped God's people when they needed it out of a hope that God would see her.

> **God cares about people. All people. No one is too far from Him.**

Not only did God see her and spare her family, but she is listed in the genealogy of Jesus that opens the book of Matthew. Traditionally, women were not listed in genealogies. Why does Matthew include two women who were not even included in the people of God—a Moabite widow named Ruth and a Canaanite prostitute named Rahab? Why include them in the honored lineage of the Son of Man who was also the Son of God?

What's going on here? What kind of a God sends His Son to seek and save the lost? What kind of a Savior goes to the house of tax collectors and prostitutes? What kind of a King suffers and dies for the people? That's the opposite of what kings do—the people are supposed to die for them, not the other way around.

What's the Bible trying to tell us? God cares about people. All people. No one is too far from Him. The last person who thinks they could be included in His plan? God loves them. He sees them. He cares for them. He rescues them.

That's His mission.

Three Stories to Make One Point

Luke 15 is one of my favorite chapters in the Bible.

Jesus tells three stories in a row: the first about a shepherd with a hundred sheep who loses one; the second about a woman with ten coins who loses one; and the third about a dad with two sons who—wait for it—loses one. Notice a trend?

In the Bible, repetition always equals emphasis. Jesus wants to make sure we see how important this is. The religious leaders are mad at Him for spending so much time around sinners. He knows this and He wants to make it abundantly clear what He's up to.

You've probably heard this third story referred to as the Parable of the Prodigal Son. Not only is it one of the most famous stories Jesus ever told, but it's also one of the most famous stories in human history.

Two guys who knew a thing or two about stories—William Shakespeare and Charles Dickens—both said it's basically a perfect story. Rembrandt, the prolific Dutch painter from the 17th century, was so moved by the story that it became the inspiration for his most famous work, *The Return of the Prodigal Son*.

Why has this story made such an impact? Because it gives us a window into God's heart. He cares about people. When one of them is lost, He doesn't stop until they come home.

Let's go back to the sheep and the shepherd. Jesus liked that metaphor. The most famous chapter in the biggest book of the Bible (Psalm 23) starts with the phrase "The Lord is my shepherd." Jesus says there's a shepherd with 100 sheep. He loses one. So what does the shepherd do? He leaves the 99 to go find the one.

When the shepherd finds the lost sheep, he calls all of his friends and neighbors for a celebration because what was lost has been found. This may sound familiar to you, but this is provocative. Jesus is being radical. He's pushing on these religious people. He's messing with them.

He tells these people—whose whole lives centered around how righteous they were in everything they said and did—that there's *more joy* in heaven over one sinner who comes home than 99 who don't need to repent.

What does God care about? What moves His heart? What is He thinking about? Lost people coming home.

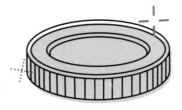

The second story is about a woman who loses one of her ten coins. Jesus basically says that she'll turn the whole house upside down until she finds it.

If you're a parent, you've probably been surprised by how easy it is for your kids to lose things. They lose their homework; they lose clothes; they lose your remote—and they won't think it's a big deal. They're not that motivated to find it. You have to tell them, "No one is doing anything until we find it."

I'm not really a dog person, but years ago when my kids were younger, they begged and pleaded to take in a rescue Golden Retriever named Kingston. He was a good boy and the whole family loved him.

My youngest daughter used to follow him everywhere and constantly snuggle him. So you can imagine her level of panic one day as a toddler when she couldn't find him. She told her siblings and my wife. I've never seen the family move so fast. Everyone was running in different directions to find Kingston.

I thought, *My family is on a mission.* They never moved this fast to find their homework, a piece of clothing, or my remote. They were going to do whatever it took to bring this lost member of the family home.

If you've lost a dog or a child (for a few minutes), you know what this is like. You feel it. It's emotional.

The Loving Father Who Is Waiting

Which brings us back to Jesus' third story in Luke 15.

There is a man with two sons. The younger son tells his dad he wants his share of the estate. In our world this may seem a little demanding or entitled on the part of the son, but in the ancient world it was far worse. You received your inheritance when your father passed, so demanding it early was the equivalent of saying, "I wish you were dead."

The father agrees and the son leaves his home and follows his own desires. The Bible says he squandered his wealth on wild living, which shows that as much as the world changes, human desires remain the same. Before long, there's a famine. He's lost everything, so he hires himself out as a servant and is fighting with the pigs he's taking care of for something to eat.

And then there's a turning point. Jesus says he comes to his senses. He sees himself and his father in a different light. He remembers how well his father treats people, and he realizes he's sinned against his dad and against heaven. He makes a plan to go home and repent to his father. He's no longer worthy to be a son but maybe he could be treated like a servant.

While he's still a long way off, his dad sees him—which is another way of saying that his dad had been thinking about him and hoping he'd come home. It goes better than this foolish son could have hoped. His dad is moved with compassion, runs out to him, throws his arms around him, and welcomes him home. He calls for a great celebration because his son who was thought dead is alive—this lost son has been found.

Jesus is summarizing God's heart for people through the love this dad has for his lost son. It should fill us with hope. It should overwhelm us with God's unconditional, never-ending love. It should move us with this grace we could never earn.

But there's another character in this story, and he puts a damper on this emotional scene. It's the older brother. Not only is he not joining in on the celebration, but he's angry. He feels violated by the injustice of it all. When the dad finds out how he's responding, he goes looking for his older son—who is now lost in a different way.

Maybe a more difficult way. The older son (like the religious leaders) thinks life is about what we earn and what we deserve. He's thinking, *I was good, so I deserve good, but you never gave me anything to celebrate with my friends. And now my idiot brother blew our money and you throw him the best party? It's not fair! He deserves punishment, not celebration.*

Sound familiar? Thousands of years later these attitudes still come naturally to us.

The father finishes the story by saying, "You've been with me the whole time and everything I have is yours. But your brother who was dead is now alive; he was lost but now he's found."

The emotion in this story is so strong. Years ago, I preached this passage and a man came up to me with tears in his eyes. It was clear he had cried throughout the service. He pulled out a picture of his son, handed it to me, and through his tears he asked, "Will you pray for my prodigal?"

In the next service I told the story and by the end of the weekend I had a pocket full of names to pray for.

We all think it's important for people who are lost to come home and give their lives to Christ. We want it to happen for everyone. Unfortunately for most of us, that's as far as we're willing to go.

But it's different when your son or daughter or grandchild is the one who is lost. You're not indifferent. You're not casual about it. This is the point of the story. The way we feel about *our* lost person is the way God feels about *every* lost person.

This requires more than general agreement. We have to be willing to serve. We have to be willing to pray. And perhaps most of all, we have to be willing to be inconvenienced.

We might not sing your favorite song. We might not cover a subject in the message you're passionate about. You might not get to sit in your same seat or keep the same Small Group forever. That's when we have to remember—it's not about us. We're joining God's mission to reach people; He's not joining our mission to make sure things are always exactly how we like them. When we act this way, we're just like the older brother.

God cares for all of His people, but His heart is always turned toward the lost son or daughter.

This story makes it abundantly clear that the mission of God is not, "Do good spiritual things to earn your rewards." There is no life down that road. The message of Jesus, the good news of the gospel, is not about making bad people good so they can earn their righteousness. It's so much better than that.

> **THE GOOD NEWS OF THE GOSPEL IS THAT THE LOST CAN BE FOUND AND THE DEAD CAN BE MADE ALIVE IN CHRIST.**

The good news of the gospel is that the lost can be found and the dead can be made alive in Christ.

How Do Broken People Reach a Perfect God?

For clarification, the term "prodigal" means "to spend lavishly." By that definition, no one spends more than the father in this story. It's all his money, his time, and his emotional energy—and all the dads know what I'm talking about!

One of the surprise twists of the Parable of the Prodigal Son is that there is not one lost son; there are two. Depending on your personality and life experience, most people tend to gravitate toward either the younger or the older son. But the truth is, we're all capable of acting like either.

The younger son is selfish and immature and does what he feels like doing. The older son is a self-righteous rule-follower who ends up angry and judgmental because he feels like no one got what they deserved.

Both paths lead to the same spot—separated from the father.

This is a problem for more than these two sons; it's the problem for all humanity. Every one of us is created in the image of God, and our deepest longing is to know and love God. But there's a problem: in order to have a relationship with a perfect God, you have to be perfect. None of us meet this standard.

If we're honest, we can admit we all have moments when we feel guilty. We don't need help to feel guilty. We feel guilty because *we are* guilty.

The world is a broken place. Real evil exists—but not just out there; it's in us too. Others have broken us, but sometimes we do the breaking. Especially in the lives of those we love most.

So what do we do? *How do broken people reach a perfect God?* There are really only three options:

① We try to be perfect.

Trying to be perfect may work for a little while, but it makes you exhausted and angry at everyone else, like the older son. I don't recommend it. It's a guaranteed way to be miserable.

② We convince ourselves God is not perfect.

Convincing ourselves God is not perfect sounds very zen and mature, but why put our hope in someone who has the same problems and character flaws we have? It defeats the purpose.

③ We find a perfect substitute.

The only option that truly works is the option Jesus provides. He offers Himself as the perfect substitute.

I was thinking about this one day in the airport as I was waiting with more than a hundred strangers slowly shuffling through the security line. Like everyone else, I was frustrated. It feels like it always takes longer than it should.

The security agents were giving their usual song-and-dance routine about shoes, laptops, and any fluid containers with more than 3.5 ounces. If you travel and pay attention, none of this is a surprise.

The whole purpose of the line is to prevent you from taking anything dangerous to yourself or others on the other side of the scanner. Sometimes the line slows down because people forget an item they know isn't allowed—scissors, a pocket knife, a water bottle. If you want to go to the other side, you've got to get rid of it.

But what if the problem is inside your heart? There is no way to get it out, and you know there is no way you'll ever pass the scan. How anxious would you be in line? How ashamed would you feel? The only way you can get through is if someone else takes your place and is scanned for you. This is what Jesus does for us.

Jesus has a perfect relationship with God. He has for eternity. He lived the perfect life we should have lived but couldn't. And yet He willingly died the death we deserved in our place to pay the debt we owed. Now through His infinite love He offers His perfect relationship with God to anyone who would receive it by faith.

I know. It seems too good to be true. That's what makes it the gospel—the good news.

"God made him who had no sin to be sin for us, so that in him we might become the righteousness of God."[1]

Righteousness is not doing enough spiritual things to earn your way to heaven. It's not your ability to outperform your heathen friends. "Righteousness" is a legal term meaning "right standing with God." It's a status that's conferred over a defendant who is on trial.

[1] 2 Corinthians 5:21

Jesus gives us His righteousness so we can have perfect peace with God to love and enjoy Him forever. We don't earn it, we don't deserve it, and we have no reason to look down on other sinners. Instead we look up to a gracious God who loved us while we were His enemies, hostile and separated from Him.

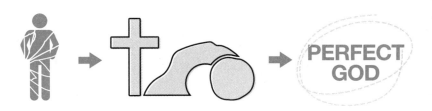

That's His mission—and He invites all of us into it with Him.

The Great "Co-mission" and the Great Commandment

God wanted to reach the whole world and He planned on using His children to do it. People who were far from God weren't to be treated as enemies, rivals, or objects but as long-lost children waiting to come home.

The word "mission" comes from the Latin word meaning "to send." Before Jesus went to be with the Father, He made one of the most defining statements in all of Scripture. It has come to be known as "the Great Commission."

> And Jesus came and said to them, "All authority in heaven and on earth has been given to me. Go therefore and make disciples of all nations, baptizing them in the name of the Father and of the Son and

of the Holy Spirit, teaching them to observe all that
I have commanded you. And behold, I am with you
always, to the end of the age."[2]

The Great Commission is a "co-mission." We do it together.
That's the whole point. God doesn't need us but He includes us
in His plan.

From God's perspective, all of His children, no matter if they've
been with Him for five decades or five minutes, are His
ambassadors. We may have different roles, but we're all called. In
fact, the role of pastors and leaders is not to do ministry while the
people watch. Ephesians 4:11-12 tells us it is the opposite:

So Christ Himself gave the apostles, the prophets,
the evangelists, the pastors and teachers, to equip His
people for works of service, so that the body of Christ
may be built up . . .

The role of pastors and leaders isn't to accomplish the mission of
God while everyone else works their job and lives their life. It's to
equip His people to serve and build the body of Christ.

When the Great Commission says "Go…" in verse 19, the tense
of the verb there is closer to "as you're going." In other words,
while you're doing your everyday things in life, make disciples.

As a Christian, my responsibility is to be equipped and do
works of service—to love my neighbors, to tell people about
Jesus, to pray for those who are discouraged and sick, and to

[2] Matthew 28:18-20, ESV

make disciples. As the lead pastor of Milestone Church, my responsibility is to equip God's people to do the work of the ministry.

This distinction is massive.

So many people come to church to watch the pastor lead, preach, and teach. They assume their role is to attend, observe, and try to remember at least a little bit about what the pastor said. While this is a common cultural idea, it's not biblical.

The job of a pastor isn't to do ministry; it's to train and develop the people to join God in His mission to reach the world through the Church.

God's mission was not to start a religion or to build an irrelevant organization. God's mission is to advance His Kingdom in the earth. And we know His Kingdom is made known when life looks the way God intended—this starts with lives being changed by entering into a genuine relationship with Jesus, but it's much more than that.

Remember, it's reaching people *and* building lives. God's Kingdom is established through His Church, not a political power or a nation. The Bible is clear that the whole earth will praise Him[3] and that His Church is made up of men and women from every tribe, tongue, and nation.[4]

God's Kingdom comes through His Church. This isn't a building; it's the people of God, His body, His family in the earth. And

---

[3] Psalms 66:4; 67:3-5; Habakkuk 2:14
[4] Revelation 7:9

the Kingdom goes wherever His people bring His love and His presence through serving and loving others.

- When a man or a woman goes to work and uses their gifts to love and serve others, the Kingdom advances.
- When a student goes to school, prays for a friend, and offers them the love of Jesus, the Kingdom advances.
- When a Small Group comes together to serve a single mom and take care of the sick, the hurting, or the poor, the Kingdom advances.

God's plan for His Church is so much bigger than a place where people gather once a week, make an individual commitment to Him, and then return to a wicked, dying world that's growing increasingly worse.

The Church was created to make an impact wherever it goes.

At the same time, the mission of God is not to simply ensure every child has all of their basic needs, a loving home in a safe community, a good education, quality health care, plenty of recreational activities, and the life of their dreams only to live selfishly and separated from God.

It's *the Great Commission*—go therefore and make disciples—and it's *the Great Commandment*—love the Lord your God with all your heart, soul, mind, and strength, and love your neighbor as yourself.[5] When they come together, the results are supernatural.

[5] Matthew 28:19-20; 22:37-40

What Keeps Us from the Mission?

You're probably thinking, *Jeff, this sounds amazing. But if God's mission is so clear and makes such an impact, why doesn't it happen more?*

Great point. I think there are several reasons why this is the case.

① We don't know the mission.

As we've discussed, church can be vague and ambiguous. I've found that many people never really understood what the goal was, so they never made progress. We've dealt with this one.

② We don't feel qualified.

This is a good starting place. Moses, David, the disciples, and nearly everyone who ended up joining God in His mission felt this way. It's like the feeling you get when you head home from the hospital with your first child. You look at your spouse and think, *Are we qualified to do this?* You're not! But as you pray and trust God, He helps you and you start to figure it out.

③ We don't know how our part fits.

Most people struggle to connect what they do every day with God's purpose and mission. But when we realize we can advance His Kingdom and join His mission "as we're going" into the normal everyday aspects of our lives, we can all do our part.

Ephesians 4:16 says the church grows and builds itself up in love as each part does its work. No one can do every part, but when all of us do our part—offer our unique contribution—the impact is incredible.

④ We're not willing to be inconvenienced.

I want to come back to Luke 15, the story of the prodigal son, and my friend who gave me a picture of his son. We all think we want to be part of a growing church. But are we willing to sacrifice? Can we care about lost people the way this father cared about his son?

Remember, that's how God feels about every person who is lost.

It's not easy being part of a growing church. Just as new members of our natural families create change, excitement, and difficulty, the same is true in our spiritual family. Things are constantly changing because new people come in with new problems and needs. We get to be part of loving and serving them.

Let me be as clear as I can possibly be: *There will always be building projects and new opportunities to give sacrificially.*

This is not because we really like building things. It's because we're really into seeing lost people come home. That's why we do it. And we can't do it without being inconvenienced.

Finding a parking spot can be more difficult. Someone might sit in "our seat." We don't keep the same Small Group forever because we need new leaders to help serve the new people who want to experience the same joy we got through finding a group and meeting friends.

> God's Kingdom comes through His Church.

Any of these can create misunderstandings and unmet expectations that can become an offense. And when an offense goes unresolved, it grows. These types of offenses are a trap the enemy uses to pull us off-mission and keep us from what God has for us.

Our Part in God's Mission

We've spent all this time talking about God's mission, His plan to establish His Kingdom and redeem the world. I know what you're thinking: *Okay, Jeff, I get it. But what can I do?*

No one can do everything, but everyone can do something. There are four things you can start doing today. Each of them will help you answer God's invitation to join His mission and change the world.

① **Love people.**

In the Great Commission, Jesus told the disciples to start in Jerusalem, then move to Judea and Samaria, and then to the ends of the earth.[6] Basically, He was telling them to start in their city, then their region, and then keep going until they covered the globe.

Because the mission of Jesus is relational, it can spread wherever there are people who love Him and love others.

Don't feel like you need to preach a sermon. Simply take a genuine interest in people. Love them the way God loves you. Listen to what they're saying—and what they're not saying. Pray for them, care about them, and tell them about what Jesus has done in your life. To do this part, you'll probably want to spend some time with Him, talk with Him about them, ask Him the best way to love them, and do what He says.

This is the biggest one. If you'll live this out, all the rest will follow. It sounds simple, but it's really difficult. It will inconvenience you.

[6] Acts 1:8

It will force you to get off the couch, to cancel your plans, to have people all up in your personal space, to go places you don't want to go, to wait, to be disappointed, and to make yourself vulnerable. If you're doing this to get credit or look spiritual, I have bad news for you. But if you're doing this because God's love is so incredible you can't think of living any other way, then you'll find His love is so much greater and more beautiful than you know.

② Pray with purpose.

I have a prayer card in my Bible that I've had since we first planted Milestone. It's filled with all kinds of requests, but on the side, there are lists of names, and many of them are crossed off. I cross off a name when the person I've been praying for gives their life to Christ. I would encourage you to do the same. It's a great reminder that our loving Father is waiting for them to come home.

One of the most important reasons to remember that God's mission works through His Church is the realization that it's not all on us. Every week in our environment, people give their lives to Christ. But it's never the result of the effort of one person. It's not all on you. When people come together from all different backgrounds and offer their gifts out of their love for God, you see Him in a different way.

I don't think it's possible to genuinely pray for someone without caring about them more, thinking about them more regularly, and seeing them from a different perspective. For that reason alone it's worth doing.

Praying for someone is one of the best ways to grow enough compassion and courage to invite them to church or to a ministry event. The enemy wants to convince you that if you invite your co-worker, neighbor, or family member, they'll never say yes. They might not. But what if they do? And what if God meets them when they come? It happens every week. We want it to happen in the lives of the people you love the most.

③ Serve with excellence.
There's nothing like coming to church with a friend, neighbor, or co-worker you've been praying for. You're hoping they like it. You're hoping they feel loved. You're hoping they make a genuine connection. And when the people serving them go above and beyond and treat them with first-class excellence, it communicates God's love in a powerful way.

Think about someone in your life who loves you, makes you a priority, and goes out of their way to put your interests ahead of their own. When they talk honestly with you, how do you respond? You listen and really take it to heart, right? Me too.

Serving people is one of the most practical ways to demonstrate the love of Jesus. You never love someone more

SERVING PEOPLE IS ONE OF THE MOST PRACTICAL WAYS TO DEMONSTRATE THE LOVE OF JESUS.

than when you take care of the people they love. They won't forget it. And when you do this in Jesus' name, it demonstrates His love and heart for them.

Every weekend across all of our campuses it takes thousands of volunteers to make this happen—people who have their own busy schedules, who have their own worries and problems, who willingly choose to offer their part so someone else can experience the love of God.

This is not a small thing—it's supernatural. It's overwhelming. And it's how God's mission happens.

④ Give generously.

If I really want to know what matters to you, I won't ask you; I'll look at your bank statement. Whatever dominates your resources is what matters most to you.

Jesus said that where your treasure is, your heart will be also.[7] It was true then and it's even more accurate today in our hyper-materialistic culture. There's no way you can say you want to join God in His mission without giving—and giving generously.

You can start these today. I've lived this way for years and I'll never stop trying to improve and mature in each of these areas—not in order for God to love me, but because He already does. I'm convinced there's no better way to live.

There's a reason you're here. You can have as much purpose and meaning in life as you're willing to embrace. You'll find it as you

[7] Matthew 6:21

join God by offering your unique gifts and resources into His mission.

It's scary and wild at first, but once you've experienced it, living any other way is boring.

KEY THOUGHTS

- God cares about people. All people. No one is too far from Him.

- God's highest priority is lost people coming home.

- How do broken people try to reach a perfect God?
    1. We try to be perfect.
    2. We convince ourselves that God is not perfect.
    3. We find a perfect substitute.

    The only option that truly works is the option Jesus provides. He offers Himself as the perfect substitute.

- Both the Great Commission—go therefore and make disciples—and the Great Commandment—love the Lord your God with all your heart, soul, mind, and strength, and love your neighbor as yourself—are our call as Christians to fulfill the mission of God.

- The Great Commission is a "co-mission." We do it together. God doesn't need us, but He includes us in His plan.

- What keeps us from the mission?
    1. We don't know the mission.
    2. We don't feel qualified.
    3. We don't know how our part fits.
    4. We aren't willing to be inconvenienced.

- Our part in God's mission:
    1. Love people.
    2. Pray with purpose.
    3. Serve with excellence.
    4. Give generously.

NEXT STEPS ✓

—Make a list of the people in your life who are far from God. Put it in your Bible and pray for them on a regular basis.

—How many of the four parts in God's mission are you participating in? What would it look like for you to take another step?

DISCIPLESHIP
IS WORTH IT

IF YOU HAD TO GUESS OUR VALUES before we started this section, I think most people would have "the Bible" and "mission" on their list. These make sense.

But what do we do with "discipleship"?

This is not a word we typically use in our daily lives. I've found that the average person knows it has something to do with church, refers to the first followers of Jesus, and might be a class or a program.

It's vague. It's not clear. And because of this, it remains relatively unimportant.

This explains why most church consultants and experts in spiritual formation cite the lack of discipleship as one of the leading reasons why people struggle to develop a meaningful relationship with God that impacts all aspects of their lives.

It was not unclear to Jesus. Remember "the Great Commission" from the last chapter? The clear target Jesus painted for His followers? The co-mission we're supposed to do together?

> In the early church, disciples were more than students; they were *apprentices*.

Jesus promised to always be with anyone willing to join Him on this mission and to give them all His authority in heaven and on Earth to accomplish the task. It's a big deal.

The whole mission was "Go and make disciples." Jesus risked the entirety of His mission to advance His Kingdom and take over the world on this one strategy: discipleship.

If this is true, and we care about fulfilling this goal, then we need to be just as clear.

What Is Discipleship?

When we hear the word "disciple," our first thought is typically a classroom or a Small Group where participants gain spiritual information. The emphasis is on teaching and spiritual content.

But in the early church, disciples were more than students; they were *apprentices*. Concepts and theories were not the goal. You weren't preparing for a presentation or an exam. You were preparing for life. You had to know how to actually do it.

Discipleship is one Christ-follower helping another Christ-follower take their next step.

You are never too young or too old. As long as you're alive and you're walking with Jesus, you're a perfect candidate.

In our world, the term "Christian" is more well-known, but from the beginning Jesus invited His followers to become disciples. It was the common term for a follower of Christ.

The Bible uses this word more than 250 times; by comparison, the word "Christian" only appears in passing three times.[1] My goal is not to discredit the value of being a Christian, but you can make the case that the term has become a catch-all for a box that gets checked by someone who nominally believes in a Judeo-Christian worldview and occasionally attends services at Easter or Christmas.

Discipleship is not a label or an ideological category. It's a vibrant and dynamic relationship. There's a greater level of commitment and a clearer connection to the mission of Christ inherent in the word.

[1] Acts 11:26b ("The disciples were called Christians first at Antioch"); Acts 26:28 (King Agrippa asks Paul, "Do you think...you can persuade me to be a Christian?"); 1 Peter 4:16 ("However if you suffer as a Christian...")

Jesus poured everything He had into His disciples over the course of His three years of ministry. He lived with them and covered every conceivable subject. But more than the concepts, He got deep into their actions, their attitudes, and even their motivations.

He's still doing the same in our lives today. His goal has not changed.

On most days, His disciples rarely understood, constantly underperformed, regularly complained about petty things, and generally missed the point. And yet He never gave up on them. He took the long view. His goal was for each of them to take the next step.

He was investing in His followers so that they, in turn, could invest in those who would come later. His entire strategy hinged on the success of this approach.

It's important to add that Jesus' emphasis on discipleship did not communicate disdain for the crowds of people who followed Him from a distance. He was moved by their needs, demonstrated compassion for them, and asked His disciples to feed them. In the same way, we love people—not just disciples. While we believe discipleship is a natural progression in the life of a follower of Christ, we do not believe it creates a hierarchy of spiritual maturity or a standard beyond simple faith in the finished work of Jesus Christ to be accepted into the people of God.

Discipleship is relational: *Watch what I do; now you do it; now we talk about how we can do it better.* None of us are ever finished. The program doesn't end. As long as we're alive, we're meant to follow Jesus and keep taking steps.

And Jesus believed the best way we learn to keep taking steps ourselves is by helping someone else take their next step. It's genius. Jesus is really smart. This is the most effective personal development strategy in existence.

Everything that's healthy grows. Healthy people grow. Healthy businesses grow. Healthy schools grow. And healthy churches grow.

I'm grateful to live in a growing area. There are a few downsides (traffic and nails in your tires), but the majority of the people in our region come because they want to grow, they want to get better, and they're motivated to become a better version of who God created them to be.

The goal is not to stay at church doing inconsequential spiritual activities. That's not discipleship. First and foremost, discipleship makes you more like Jesus. You see people the way He sees them. You love what He loves. You honor God in the way you serve and care for people.

Because this is true, it impacts every facet of your life—your character at work, the way you treat your spouse, how you train

AS LONG AS WE'RE ALIVE, WE'RE MEANT TO FOLLOW JESUS AND KEEP TAKING STEPS.

EVERYTHING
THAT'S HEALTHY
GROWS. HEALTHY
PEOPLE GROW.
HEALTHY
BUSINESSES
GROW. HEALTHY
SCHOOLS GROW.
AND HEALTHY
CHURCHES
GROW.

your children, the way you relate to your neighbor and even people who disagree with everything you value.

This is the heart of discipleship; it's a person, not a class. Discipleship is also a seed—it never stops growing and consistently bears fruit that over time bears its own fruit.

What Keeps People from Discipleship?

Acts 6:7 tells us that the Word of God spread and the number of disciples in Jerusalem increased rapidly. Jesus' strategy works. But if that's true, why is it not more common in our world today?

① They can't see it.

Quite simply, I believe the biggest issue is a lack of clarity. They think it's a class. They think it's a deep dive into super-spiritual concepts for a select few. They don't understand how it impacts every area of their lives, so they're open to the idea of it, but it remains an aspirational value as opposed to an actual one.

The other issue is that they're distracted by other things. I have met hundreds of well-meaning Christian people who are convinced Jesus' strategy is a deeper understanding of the end times, political activism and engagement, the agendas of nonprofit organizations, or the latest technological innovation that could allow us to retell the gospel in new ways.

I'm not suggesting that any of these interests are bad, but I have a hard time seeing how they take a higher priority than the thing Jesus asked us to do: make disciples.

② They feel unprepared.

Look, I get it. Who doesn't feel unqualified or unprepared for the simple task of accomplishing Jesus' mission in the earth? But we seem to be way more nervous about this than Jesus was. He was quick to put His disciples in the game, to give them responsibility, to allow them to learn on the job.

He was not expecting either perfect candidates or perfect outcomes. Two of the most critical leaders in the early church, Peter and Paul, had less than stellar reputations as a result of their personal challenges. They never would have survived "cancel culture."

Peter consistently blew it and denied Jesus when He needed him most. Before Saul was the apostle Paul, he was Saul the religious expert who killed Christians. And yet no two followers of Christ were more instrumental in making disciples and advancing the mission.

No responsible parent ever feels fully up to the job, but we do our best anyway. The same is true when it comes to making disciples.

③ They're not willing to obey.

This is the toughest of the three obstacles. This person understands how important it is, and they believe they can do it, but they choose not to because they'd rather follow their own desires than follow Jesus.

The heart of God is really big and His love is so much bigger than we can grasp. In our passion for His mission and our excitement for the benefits that come from discipleship, we can't confuse how our relationship with God works. Discipleship does not make us right with God. The theological term for this is "justification." None of us are restored to a relationship with God on the basis of our ability to follow. We receive the righteousness of Jesus as a free gift from God—we can't earn it and we don't deserve it.

This justification happens in a moment. But this moment is followed by a process where our character is changed and we become more and more of who God created us to be. This is the process of discipleship, and the theological term is "sanctification." It's how we grow.

Growth requires intentionality and effort. It's not easy. We have to keep taking steps. We have to die to ourselves. We have to choose not to follow our feelings in order to follow Jesus. I wish I could say everyone was motivated and inspired to do this, but it's not the case. God is so patient and loving, and because He always has our best in mind, our lack of obedience does not mean these people "get away" with anything. The saddest part is, they're the ones who miss out.

In those circumstances, we keep praying and asking God to change their hearts.

How Does Discipleship Work?

I'm praying that as you're reading this, you're now thinking, *Okay, Jeff, you convinced me. I'm in. I want to do it. But if it's relational, not a class or a program, what do I do?*

Excellent question. Why do we have to make disciples? Because they don't make themselves.

The first step you have to take is the choice to be a disciple, which is also the choice to make disciples. In other words, you're not truly the first part . . . until you've done the second part.

Paul's letters to Timothy (a young pastor leading a big church in Ephesus) give us a great window into the discipleship process. In 2 Timothy 2:2, Paul gives one of the clearest and most important summaries into how this works:

> And the things you have heard me say in the presence
> of many witnesses entrust to reliable people who will
> also be qualified to teach others.

In this one little verse we see a window into Jesus' brilliant strategy. "Be a disciple" is always connected to "make a disciple." This is the heart of discipleship. This is how it works.

Think about this...there are five groups of disciples in this one verse:

1. The people who taught Paul
2. Paul
3. Timothy
4. Reliable people
5. Others

Every time we take our next step in our walk with Jesus, baked into the process is the step of helping someone else take their next step.

We teach what we know, but we reproduce what we are.

It's more about our actions, attitudes, and motivation than information. Paul told the Corinthians, "Follow my example as I follow the example of Christ." The key word in the sentence is "Christ." This is not about our style or personality. We're not making disciples of ourselves but of Christ.

How Do I Know If I'm a Disciple?

I want this to be even more practical. Over the years, I've had moments when someone who I've been meeting with regularly will ask me, "When does the discipleship start?" The question always makes me laugh a little. "What do you think we've been doing?"

For the sake of clarity, here's how you can tell someone is a disciple.

① I commit to an ongoing relationship with Jesus <u>and</u> the people He's called me to.

Discipleship happens along the way in day-to-day life. When Jesus chose the disciples in Mark 3:14, before sending them out to preach, He chose them *to be with Him.* You prioritize being with Jesus and the key relationships He brings to your life. It's more demonstration than explanation.

It's more than a personal advisor who signs off on your choices, a personal priest who spiritualizes everything, or a friend who encourages you no matter what you decide. You commit to a lifestyle: *This is how I'm going to live moving forward. I posture myself in a way where Jesus can speak to any issue in my life at any time. And I realize He often does this through people.*

② I commit to identifiable growth.

None of us become like Jesus overnight. But like any relationship, the more time we spend with someone, the more we talk and think like they do.

Over the course of the last several decades, I've watched the personal-growth industry explode. I've benefited from so many aspects of it. K. Anders Ericsson popularized the idea of 10,000 hours of intentional practice in order to hit peak performance. Carol Dweck demonstrated how the key step in growth is moving from a fixed mindset (this is all I'll ever be) to a growth mindset (I can change and improve).

But we grow when we have clear metrics and track outcomes. We count steps, calories, and other quantifiable growth. This can be tricky when it comes to our spiritual growth, but the general principles apply.

In 1 Timothy 4:15, Paul tells Timothy to be diligent in these areas, to give everything he has to his growth, so that everyone can see his progress.

- Are you reading your Bible and growing in your understanding of God's Word?
- Are you regularly experiencing God's presence through your prayer life and times of worship?
- Do the people closest to you see growth in your character and the way you love and serve others?

- Are you using your gifts to serve others through your connection to spiritual family?
- Are you reproducing what God is doing in you in someone else?

The specific details of these will look different depending on the season of life, but each of these is a clear sign of progress in the life of a disciple. This doesn't mean we don't have setbacks and opportunities for coaching. It's all part of the process.

③ I commit to receive with the right heart.

Disciples are teachable. They're not arrogant or filled with pride. They posture themselves as learners. They're not people pleasers; they're humble and they want to grow. They're not defensive; they receive coaching and correction with a heart of gratitude.

When we find these kinds of people in our workplace or in our families, we all think the same thing: *I love being around them!*

Disciples aren't perfect but they are life-giving. They add value to every environment they're in. The Bible says we often find out whether a person is wise or a fool once they're corrected.[2]

In our world, people often overreact when they're corrected. This is especially hard on young people—they're inclined to receive correction as rejection. They have to navigate the difficult line of forging their own identity while seeking the affirmation of their peers. But in Hebrews 12 the Bible reminds us that discipline or correction from God is a sign of His love, not of His anger or lack of approval.

[2] Proverbs 9:8-9; 17:10

Correction and healthy conflict are small parts of the discipleship process, but few things give us a more accurate picture of our maturity and emotional health.

How Do You Make Disciples?

If Jesus believed you had to be a disciple to make disciples, how does that part work? All of us become like the people we listen to and spend time with. Discipleship starts with finding a candidate. When people get excited about discipleship, one of the first questions they ask me is "Where do you find one?"

If you're a parent, the first place to look is in your home. The most important disciples you'll ever make live under your roof. You don't just raise children; you train them. You can't force your kids to be disciples, but it's your responsibility to inspire and invite them into the process.

Beyond your home you're not looking for someone who is sitting around with nothing better to do. Jesus didn't do this. He called groups of brothers to leave their fishing business. He went to tax collectors and religious experts. He went to doctors and people who had full lives. He saw in each of them a measure of leadership, the capacity to commit to something bigger than themselves, and a willingness to grow.

① Get someone.

Look first in your home. Then look in the places you're already spending your time (work, church, Small Group, hobbies, etc.). Ask God to show you someone who has a desire to grow in their relationship with God and understands the value of personal development.

② Be with them.

It's not a class or a program; it's a relationship. It doesn't work if you don't spend time with them. Giving someone our time is one of the greatest expressions of value we can offer, especially as our responsibilities and demands grow. Jesus consistently spent time with the disciples because attitudes, perspectives, and character issues only surface when you're around people.

This can happen in a Small Group over a meal, one on one while you're enjoying a hobby or working on a project, or in a conference room during a break at the office. In other words, in the normal, everyday moments of life.

③ Help them in the basics.

Begin at the beginning. Help them to read and receive from the Word. Discuss the Bible with them. You don't have to be an expert; you simply need to be growing and learning yourself. Help them develop a prayer life. Help them grow in their character and the way they love and serve people, starting in their home with their closest relationships.

④ Challenge and encourage them.

We don't grow in our comfort zone. We need inspiration and encouragement. Help them identify and move toward their next step. The recipe always includes a mix of honest dialogue, prayerful reflection, patient understanding, inspiration, and challenge. You won't always have the answers, but you can always share your experience and offer to pray, and ask God to help you keep moving forward.

Be interested in their lives. Don't just make small talk. Point them back to the Word. Make it safe for them to be honest. Listen actively. Ask follow-up questions. It takes time to develop trust but the impact is significant. Text them and encourage them when they have a big meeting/project at work or something happening in their family.

What Happens When We Live This Way?

Ron and Azu

Ron was invited to Milestone by a friend many times before he finally showed up. He was married with a young daughter, and like so many other men in our area, he was experiencing all the things the world promised would lead to fulfillment; he was living the American dream. And somehow, *it wasn't enough*. He found himself wanting more.

This led to a series of bad choices that threatened the future of his marriage.

Ron grew up faithfully attending church, but by the time he got to college he had stopped going. He didn't have a personal relationship with Jesus, and he certainly wasn't a disciple. With his home life collapsing, he went home and held his daughter. As he laid her back down in her bed, he came to the conclusion that he couldn't live this way any longer. He walked out of his home and moved in with relatives in the area. Not long after, his wife and daughter moved in with her parents.

From all appearances it looked as though this would be the painful end of this season of his life—but the story wasn't over. What happened next was nothing short of miraculous.

In his brokenness he gave his life to Christ, but he realized there was no guarantee it would be in time to save his marriage. The divorce process was well underway, and for the next six months his wife watched closely to see if the transformation was real. Ron continued to throw himself into the Word; he served anyone he could and he demonstrated a genuine hunger to be a disciple.

In time, his wife came and gave her life to Christ, their marriage was restored, and their family has grown to include three beautiful children. As they both continued to grow in their relationship with Jesus, they served others and looked to be an encouragement to those with similar stories.

Eventually Ron joined our team and became a pastor—both he and his wife, Azu, have served in a variety of roles, but at each step they've served people through this process of discipleship. They were sent from our Keller Campus to launch a new campus in Haslet, where they both continue to develop and disciple people—helping them to take their next step following Christ.

> Because someone took the time to invite Ron into a relationship with Jesus and the people God called him to walk with, not only was his family changed but also the hundreds of people they've impacted. It's actually bigger than that. Because many of the people Ron and Azu helped take their next step helped someone else . . . who helped someone else . . .

This is the power of discipleship.

Discipleship is not a system, it's not a book, and it's not a class. Two thousand years later, it still works the same way: one follower of Christ helping another to take their next step. That's the target. I want to encourage you to try it.

We may help make them, but every disciple belongs to Jesus. He's the One who redeems, transforms, and makes them new. He's the One who gets the glory.

KEY THOUGHTS

- Discipleship is one Christ-follower helping another Christ-follower take their next step. It's for everyone.

- Discipleship is relational: *Watch what I do; now you do it; now we talk about how we can do it better.*

- What keeps people from discipleship?
    1. They can't see it.
    2. They feel unprepared.
    3. They're not willing to obey.

- "Be a disciple" is always connected to "make a disciple." This is the heart of discipleship.

- How do I know if I'm a disciple?
    1. I commit to an ongoing relationship with Jesus and the people He's called me to.
    2. I commit to identifiable growth.
    3. I commit to receiving with the right heart.

- How do you make disciples?
    1. Get someone.
    2. Be with them.
    3. Help them in the basics.
    4. Challenge and encourage them.

- You won't always have the answers but you can share your experience and offer to pray, and ask God to help you keep moving forward.

- The process has not changed. Every disciple belongs to Jesus. He's the One who redeems, transforms, and makes them new. He's the One who gets the glory.

NEXT STEPS ✓

—Make it a goal this month to take a next step in your walk with Christ. This may include getting in the Growth Track (Discovery 101, Serve Team 201, or Values 301) or joining or leading a Small Group.

—Seek out someone in your spiritual family who can help you as you grow in your Christian walk. No matter how far along we are in our relationship with Christ, we all need trusted voices and anchor points to help us continue to develop.

—Remember, every follower in Christ can make disciples. Start with the people around you and ask yourself, "Who needs to be developed?" Plan a meeting and get started!

9
SPIRITUAL FAMILY IS WORTH IT

IF YOU'VE BEEN PAYING ATTENTION, you've seen me use the phrase "spiritual family" repeatedly throughout the book.

You may not have a clear sense of what this means. If I were you, I probably wouldn't get it either. Spiritual family was not something I remember hearing when I was first learning about church.

But I can't describe Milestone Church without it. And I want to make sure you know what it means because I believe it's one of the most important things about us. I'm convinced, more than any of our values, spiritual family is the one that surprises people. It catches them off guard.

When we talked about how people would consistently tell us about how they were impacted by our intentionality, our authenticity, and our sincerity, I think what they were describing is the result of a group of people committed to this value.

Only spiritual family makes this real.

But I also want to be crystal clear—this is not unique to Milestone Church. We didn't come up with it. It's not our idea. We believe spiritual family is a reflection of God's heart for people.

This is why I spend so much time and energy shaping the way we think about church. If church is like an event where people come to get spiritual content, it changes our expectations of what church can provide. If church is cause-driven and focused on addressing critical issues for subsets of the population, this shapes our ability to engage and contribute.

> **We believe spiritual family is a reflection of God's heart for people.**

If church is a religious organization, it's natural for us to relate to it as a consumer. We treat it the same way we do all the different organizations we look to in order to meet the needs of our family—our school, our grocery store, our gym, our doctor/dentist, and many other services.

We know what these relationships are like. We're looking for maximum value *and* maximum convenience. Our loyalty and commitment follow the best deal.

Many people approach their local church with the same level of commitment with which they purchase their groceries: *I'm going with whoever gives me the best deal.*

- Who has the best play area for my kids with the shortest lines and state-of-the-art retinal scans for my children? And don't forget, the Goldfish snacks must be organic *and* gluten-free.
- How many weeks do I have to wait before I can sing on the platform?
- When are you going to give the message on the seven keys for making all my dreams come true? And I want them all to start with the same letter.
- Do they have a petting zoo with live animals? Because I heard that another church in the area has that.
- How long will it take me to get a parking spot, a cup of coffee, and a seat close enough for me to see everything, yet near enough to an exit so I can sneak out early and beat the traffic?

I'm not trying to be harsh, but I didn't pull these out of thin air. They're all based on real stories. This is where so many people live.

The problem is, this approach doesn't produce much in terms of fulfillment, joy, and meaningful relationships. It's a shortsighted strategy. The convenience is helpful in the moment, but in the long run it ends up changing us.

It's like parents with small kids and their relationship with screens. The kids want the screens all the time. And when you're busy and preoccupied with other things, the screen can be a lifesaver because it gives you extra margin. We've all done it. But there are unintended consequences.

The next time you try to enjoy a family movie together or gather everyone for game night, the kids are upset because they want their screens and the freedom to watch only what they want. Choosing the freedom to watch whatever you want is also the choice not to share your experiences with the people closest to you.

As a pastor, I see how our conveniences, especially through technology, continue to impact us. We've never been more digitally connected, and yet there's never been more "crowded loneliness." We're around all kinds of people but we feel like no one really sees us and knows what's happening in our lives.

Studies have found the average person has more than 300 Facebook friends and yet more than 25 percent of that same group say they don't have a single friend who they can talk to about life's most important issues.

Social media has created a world where we know what all of our friends are eating and where they're going on vacation, but no one knows what's really happening in our lives. This only makes us feel more isolated.

I'm not anti-technology. Our devices can be wonderful tools. But this isn't how God designed us to live. We're created to be placed in a family.

Environments matter. We do everything we can to give every person who visits Milestone Church the opportunity to hear from God and experience His presence.

The most common feedback we receive at our events for people who are new to Milestone is, "We felt so welcomed. Everyone here is so friendly." By the grace of God, this isn't a coincidence.

The thousands of volunteers who show up and serve across all our campuses do their absolute best to provide excellent service. But they're not doing it for a business. They do it because they love Jesus and they're hoping through their service someone else will learn to love Him too.

Customer-service principles can create a friendly environment but they can't produce that. Only a spiritual family can make this real for people.

WHEN WE LOOK ACROSS THE BIG STORY OF THE BIBLE, GOD ALWAYS STARTS WITH A FAMILY.

Family: God's Basic Building Block

When we look across the big story of the Bible, God always starts with a family. Family expresses His character, His nature, and the way He builds. More than anything else, Adam and Eve are an extension of God's family. They were His children designed to enjoy this good world He made to be together with them.

And because the family is so central to God's pattern, these relationships became the strategic target for the enemy. His plans haven't changed. He always concentrates and incites his forces to destroy families because that's how God builds.

Before long, humanity became so broken that God hit the reset button with the flood. What was God's plan for a fresh start? He made a relationship with a man named Noah and his family (see Genesis 6-9).

It didn't take long before mankind ended up in the ditch again at the Tower of Babel (see Genesis 11). How did God respond? He found a faithful but childless old man named Abram and promised to be his God and to give him as many descendants as the stars in the sky or the sand in the desert. God changed his name to Abraham and 25 years later, at the age of 100, he became the father to Isaac (see Genesis 12-21).

While we see this pattern expressed through natural families, the principle is so central to who God is, it didn't stop there. As the biblical narrative unfolds, God formed strategic new families through bringing people from different backgrounds, nations, and cultures and placing them together in divine covenant relationships.

The Bible describes it this way in Psalm 68:5-6a: "Father to the fatherless, defender of widows—this is God, whose dwelling is holy. God places the lonely in families…"[1] This is a critical concept. I don't know about you, but I didn't choose my family. It wasn't an option. I was placed into it.

---

[1] NLT

God places us in His family.

One of the best examples of this is the story of Ruth. There's a famine in Israel, so a family leaves in search of bread. Not only do a husband, a wife, and their two sons find food in Moab, but the young men take wives and start new families of their own. But before long the father and his sons die. Now Naomi, the Israelite widow, is left to care for these two young Moabite widows.

Naomi tells these young ladies to go back to their families. The first one does the sensible thing and returns, but Ruth does something truly remarkable. Ruth has a conviction from the God of Israel. She's experiencing something more important than the need for safety and security. She tells her mother-in-law, Naomi, "Don't urge me to leave you or to turn back from you. Where you go I will go, and where you stay I will stay. Your people will be my people and your God my God. Where you die I will die, and there I will be buried. May the Lord deal with me, be it ever so severely, if even death separates you and me."[2]

What's happening here? Is Ruth being co-dependent and clingy? Not really. Naomi senses that the most likely outcome for them is death and starvation. This was not the smart play. This was not risk aversion. This was not a transactional relationship. Ruth uses covenantal language out of a conviction from God.

Ruth believes God has supernaturally placed them together and so she chooses to obey Him. God saves Ruth and Naomi. Not only do they make it back to Israel, but they find food and

---

[2] Ruth 1:16-17

connect with a man named Boaz. He's the son of a prostitute God spared from the destruction of Jericho. In a love story too crazy for even the Hallmark Channel, they end up together. And within a few generations, they have a great-grandson who the Bible describes as a man after God's own heart.

His name is David and he becomes the second king of Israel.

David was more than a descendant of Ruth; he carried the same value for spiritual family. You see, before he can become king he's forgotten by his dad and his brothers on the most important day in family history. The prophet has come to their home to choose the next king and they all forget about David. But Samuel the prophet says he's the one.

David loves God and he loves to worship. The current king is tormented, but when David plays the harp, he feels better. The king (named Saul) likes how it makes him feel but he gets really angry when all the people of Israel cheer for David after he kills an evil giant who was mocking their army.

King Saul hates David so intensely that he repeatedly tries to kill him. But in a crazy twist in the story, David finds help from the most unlikely source—the rightful heir to the throne, Saul's son Jonathan. Just like Ruth and Naomi, David and Jonathan believe God has placed them together in spiritual family. The king thinks this is crazy and he mocks them both, but they won't change their minds.

As we move through the Old Testament, we come to the story of the prophet he. God does incredible things in and through Elijah but he spends much of his life discouraged and isolated.

Then God brings him spiritual family through a protege named Elisha. Because we're designed for covenant relationships, Elijah's relationship with Elisha brings comfort in a way that some of the most dramatic miracles in the Bible could not produce.

Spiritual Family in the New Testament

Perhaps the best picture of this in the entire Bible is Jesus and His disciples. While Jesus loved and cared for His natural family (His mother, Mary, His younger brother James, and His cousin John the Baptist were all leaders in the earliest days of the Christian faith), He prioritized His relationships with spiritual family. He believed anyone who did the will of God was His brother and sister.

On the same night He would be betrayed, arrested, beaten, and eventually crucified, Jesus gathered His disciples and gave them some of the most direct insights into this concept. He told them they didn't choose Him but He chose them. He told them He loved them the same way the Father loved Him. He called them His friends and told them that there's no greater love than to lay down your life for your friends.

And then He said the whole world would know they loved Him by the way they loved each other. This is covenant language. This is how God places us in family. This is spiritual family.

Even as Jesus was dying on the cross, He looked at His mom and then He looked at His friend John and basically told them, "This is your son . . . this is your mom . . . take care of each other."[3]

---

[3] John 19:26-27

God places us in divine relationships, and the way we love and serve these people is a direct reflection of our love for God.

This made such an impression on the disciples that they built the early church on this conviction. They followed the pattern Jesus gave them, and as the gospel spread and churches were planted, men and women in Christ called each other brothers and sisters. Paul told Timothy to treat older men and women as if they were members of his own family.[4]

Because of this conviction, they put their lives at risk for each other, loved each other, served each other, cared for people who persecuted them, demonstrated a love greater than shared interests, and turned the ancient world upside down.

Paul called Timothy his true son in the faith.[5] Paul didn't think this was something unique to their relationship. He called the people in the church at Corinth his children. He said, even if they had thousands of teachers or guardians, they didn't have many fathers, but he became their father through the gospel (1 Corinthians 4:15).

The Bible makes this concept of placement so clear in 1 Corinthians 12:18: "But in fact God has placed the parts in the body, every one of them, just as he wanted them to be." We don't join a church based on convenience. God places us in His body—right where He wants us.

Not only did these relationships advance the cause of Christ and

[4] 1 Timothy 5:1-2
[5] 1 Timothy 1:2

WE DON'T JOIN A CHURCH BASED ON CONVENIENCE. GOD PLACES US IN HIS BODY— RIGHT WHERE HE WANTS US.

change the history of the world, but they also created greater personal fulfillment. Toward the end of his life, John said he had no greater joy than to hear that his children were walking in truth.[6] This is how we're designed to live. These relationships aren't easy. They come at a high cost, require a great investment, and consistently require us to defer our preferences and desires. But there is nothing like it.

The modern notion that we're the masters of our fate, we're an island unto ourselves, and we're to be true to ourselves above all has no power to produce these results.

What Prevents People from Experiencing Spiritual Family?

If this is how God builds and it's so foundational to the way we've been created to live, then why is it uncommon? Why don't more people experience the power of spiritual family? What keeps us from spiritual family?

① They lack conviction.

This concept may not be widely understood, but like the treasure buried in the field, the fact that we don't see it doesn't make it any less valuable. You get the sense the disciples never really got over how incredible this idea was. John was one of Jesus' best friends, but this incredible privilege of being adopted into God's family moved him deeply. Near the end of his life John wrote, "See what great love the Father has lavished on us that we should be called children of God! And that is what we are!"[7]

---

[6] 3 John 1:4
[7] 1 John 3:1a

Two sentences, two exclamation points. It's too good to be true. It's beyond what we could hope or imagine. God doesn't just forgive us, save us, and rescue us from our sin—He places us in His family!

Spiritual family is not about chemistry or shared interest. It's a clear conviction from God that He's divinely placed us in relationship with a body of believers.

② They've experienced family pain.

I understand some of you cringe when you hear the word "family." For you, this word doesn't produce cherished memories. Instead, it brings to mind pain and drama you're trying to get as far away from as possible. Trust me; I get it.

I've worked with people long enough to realize how painful this area of our lives can be. Because they know us so well and they're so close to us, no one can hurt us like our family. If this has been your journey, I'm self-aware enough to realize this talk about spiritual family can sound naive and idealistic.

However, no family is beyond God's reach. I've had the opportunity to watch God redeem and restore all kinds of family dysfunction. He saves marriages, restores brokenness between parents and children, heals wounds between siblings, calls the prodigal home, and restores self-righteous older brothers.

God's vision for your family is always meant to bless you, to encourage you, to inspire you, to give you the power to forgive freely, to love deeply, and to fill your home with His presence. He wants this for your family because it's the culture of His family.

③ Spiritual family is countercultural.

It's always been difficult and against the grain of human nature, but it may be more challenging today than ever before. The combination of social mobility, technological innovation, and radical individualism has created a unique cocktail that prioritizes personal freedom at the expense of our most cherished relationships.

In other words, we're more selfish and narcissistic than ever before. And our culture at large celebrates it.

Every day, in all kinds of ridiculous ways, the siren song of culture tells us to follow our hearts. Don't like your job? Leave it and go find something you're passionate about where they will value you. Having trouble with your marriage? Feeling like you love them but you're not *in* love with them? Then you owe it to yourself to go find your soulmate.

We have an infinite number of options, and technology gives us the feeling that the better version of life is one click away. We have to take control. We're in charge. We can have whatever we're willing to reach out and take.

It sounds so inspiring. It's easy to write a blog or a book about this because you never have to deal with the consequences. As a pastor, I don't have that luxury. I see what these attitudes do to people.

I've watched so many people uproot themselves in pursuit of a promotion, a new hobby/interest, or opportunities for their kids, while assuming they can easily replace their network of support relationships. They end up drifting. They hope social media will allow them to quickly form new connections until they realize digital relationships may start quickly but often struggle to move beyond surface conversations.

As a culture, there's been a shift in how we think about family. I've seen that word used to describe work, school, and even sports teams. I appreciate wanting to create a sense of belonging and connection, but you can't find a biblical precedent for this.

To satisfy this need, there's been a big push for the importance of "community." Many churches promote this as one of the primary things they provide. I understand what they're trying to do, but it bothers me.

"Community" is a vague and nondescript buzzword. It doesn't really mean anything. You can have community at your favorite coffee shop, the gym, your book club, or the guys you play fantasy football with. What you're really saying is that in one aspect of your life you've made some acquaintances because you have a few shared interests.

I don't think this is what the Bible means when it talks about spiritual family.

④ They prioritize personal freedom.

Consumer culture is rampant in our world. From the time we're very young, we're trained to look for the maximum benefit at the lowest personal cost. It's not possible to be healthy in our relationships if we carry over this same attitude.

People who constantly treat everyone in their lives as a means to their end erode trust and run out of relational capital. If every interaction centers on what people can do for you, eventually everyone in your life will distance themselves from you.

I understand why people come in and sit on the back row, keep people at a distance, come to church once a month if they're not busy doing something else, and maybe watch part of a message online. This fits with a busy lifestyle. But it won't help you go through one of life's big moments and it can't help you if you really want to grow spiritually.

That requires more. It requires spiritual family.

How Does Spiritual Family Work?

If you're still reading along, I'm hoping you're asking this question: "Okay, Jeff, you've convinced me to keep moving forward. So what do I do? How does this work?"

① You believe God has placed you in spiritual family. From the very beginning of Milestone (when we were desperate for anybody who would come), I've always told people, "I'd rather have you join Jesus than join Milestone." The reason I'm so confident in this is because I really believe God places all the parts in the body where He wants them.

We're certainly not the only church who believes in this principle. Every family has its unique strengths and weaknesses. Every family

has distinctives, special giftings, and the ability to connect and reach different types of people. That's why we're all part of the larger body of Christ. We need each other in order to reach the world.

At the same time, we work hard as a team to make it possible for as many people as we can to experience spiritual family at all our campuses. But more than liking the worship, the preaching, the friendly people, or the life-giving environment, we want you to feel that God has placed you in the church.

I've found that when people believe this, God becomes more real. Their commitment to the person sitting next to them goes way up: *This isn't a stranger; this person is part of my family.* They see their contribution as being more significant. It changes everything.

② You discover and develop your gifts in family.

I know this is a missing ingredient for so many people. They've never even thought about it. When you realize that you've come to church to play the game rather than just sit in the stands, it changes you.

Family is the most natural environment for growth and development. It's what families do. In a family you discover interests, receive feedback and coaching, provide support and opportunities, and develop talents and abilities. The process takes time and patience, but the ongoing commitment provides the proximity and honesty we all need to genuinely grow.

> Family is the most natural environment for growth and development.

This growth happens after we've committed to the family. In a healthy family, no one sits back and watches.

None of us grow when we're constantly reevaluating our commitment level and considering our options. This is true in the classroom, the workplace, the gym, the home, and definitely in the church. It's not about you; it's about all of the yous together. When any part of the family wins, every part of the family celebrates.

③ **You lean in when challenges come.**

Every family experiences moments of joy and moments of sorrow. When things are going great, it's not difficult to be gracious and loving. But when storms and challenges come—and they always do—we discover a more accurate picture of the health of our relationships.

What happens when you get offended? How do you respond to a misunderstanding? Will you still love your church when they don't emphasize the things that are deeply important to you? What if you have a problem with a Small Group leader or you're upset about the way something was handled with one of your kids?

How do you respond then?

- Will your emotions get the best of you, or will you wait for more understanding before forming your conclusions?
- Are you capable of staying open to the possibility you don't have all the information?
- Will you project the pain of previous experiences onto someone who's given you no reason to doubt their character?
- Are you willing to go straight to the person with grace

and trust, choosing to believe the best about their intentions?

I realize these are incredibly high standards. These are unusual expectations. But I know how much you'll benefit from choosing this path.

Unfortunately, I also know what happens when you take the other road. Relationships can be fractured. Faith can be injured. Offenses can create wedges between people.

I've seen people so emotional that they never take the time to learn what happened. I've watched as others decided to only listen to information that lined up with what they already believed to be true because they were more interested in being right than in making things right.

Sometimes it's the result of emotions, hurts, or offenses. Other times it's an attack from the enemy. Often it's an understandable response to an unusually challenging season. But in these difficult moments, I'm convinced there's no greater way to navigate than spiritual family.

Proverbs 27:6a says that the wounds of a friend can be trusted. Our friends, our most trusted voices, don't always tell us what we want to hear; they tell us what we *need* to hear. They love us enough to give us the truth. Proverbs 17:17 tells us a friend loves at all times, and a brother is born for adversity.

God places us in spiritual family because when the storms of life come (and they always do), it's too late to decide who we're going to trust or to find someone new who lines up with what we've already decided.

We all move toward the picture we have in our head. I'm so grateful for the fathers (both natural and spiritual) who helped me understand what really matters. As I look ahead toward the end of my life, this value of spiritual family helps to remind me of where I'm going.

My dream for my last days is to be surrounded by the people God placed in my life, both natural and spiritual, who tell me, "Well done. You ran your race. You played your part. We'll take it from here."

I've had the privilege of being a part of these moments. This is the legacy my dad handed to me. In those moments, there's nothing more important. You may think, *I've never seen anything like this. That seems impossible.*

It doesn't happen all at once. It's the result of small choices we make to love and serve the people God places in our lives the way we love and serve Him. I believe as we continue to value spiritual family, we'll continue to experience the blessings it provides in ways that will surprise us.

KEY THOUGHTS

- Spiritual family is a reflection of God's heart for people. Family expresses His character, His nature, and the way He builds. God always starts with family.

- God places us in His family right where He wants us (see Psalm 68:5-6a and 1 Corinthians 12:18).

- God places us in divine relationships, and the way we love and serve these people is a direct reflection of our love for God.

- What prevents people from experiencing spiritual family?
    1. They lack conviction.
    2. They've experienced family pain.
    3. Spiritual family is countercultural.
    4. They prioritize personal freedom.

- How does spiritual family work?
    1. You believe God has placed you in spiritual family.
    2. You discover and develop your gifts in family.
    3. You lean in when challenges come.

- Family is the most natural environment for growth and development.

- God places us in spiritual family so that when the storms of life come, we have family to lean into; it's too late to find a trusted voice after the storm hits.

NEXT STEPS ✓

—The culture of God's family is built around love, humility, forgiveness, and honor. Write down one tangible way you can strive to support each of these values within your own church and family this month.

—Reach out to five people in your spiritual family this week. Encourage them and tell them you notice and honor their contributions.

10
GENEROSITY IS WORTH IT

LOOK CAREFULLY AT VALUE #5. It's not money; it's generosity. Churches often have a reputation for being overly concerned about money. Money is a resource. Generosity is an attitude toward life.

Studies have shown that generous people are healthier, enjoy a higher quality of life, and even live longer than those who lack this quality.

When you study the Bible, it's immediately clear that God wants us to be generous. Because we're made in His image, He wants us to follow His lead and live this way.

WE'RE NEVER MORE LIKE JESUS THAN WHEN WE'RE GENEROUS. PERHAPS MORE IMPORTANTLY, YOU CAN'T BE LIKE JESUS WITHOUT BEING GENEROUS.

If most people know one verse in the Bible, it's John 3:16: "For God so loved the world He gave His only Son . . ."[1] What does God do? He gives. Why does He do it? Because He loves the world deeply.

Remember, we want these values to be actual, not aspirational. We don't want to aspire to be generous; we want to actually live this way.

I believe we're never more like Jesus than when we're generous. Perhaps more importantly, you can't be like Jesus without being generous.

It's who He is. Jesus was the one who said, "It's more blessed to give than to receive."[2]

This issue is really important to God. He's not scared to talk about money. The Bible is filled with commands, promises, and wisdom for how to faithfully handle money and use it in a way that honors God.

Jesus consistently talked about money because He believed there was a clear

---

[1] ESV
[2] Acts 20:35

connection between our treasure and our heart.³ If you want to know what's in one, look in the other.

This is why Jesus talked about money—He wants us to see what's happening in our hearts. That's what He's really after.

One of His favorite teaching techniques were parables—a simple story that creates a premise that allows us to see ourselves in a different light when we compare ourselves with the story. Many of His parables start with a similar setup: A king or a master gives resources to his servants before he leaves; then he comes back to see what they've done with what they've been given.

Jesus loved this setup because it's a timeless way to think about life. It remains as true for us today as it was on the day when Jesus told this to the crowds following Him.

From the Bible's perspective, *everything* belongs to God. He owns everything; but because He's generous, He gives freely to each of us. We're not owners; we're all stewards—managers of what we've been entrusted with. Psalm 24:1 tells us, "The earth is the Lord's, and everything in it, the world, and all who live in it."

³ Matthew 6:21

There's a prominent cultural narrative that tells us we're self-made, the captains of our fate, the masters of our destiny. We can have whatever we want if we want it bad enough and are willing to work for it. We like this story because it makes us feel strong. The only problem is, it's not true.

Without God we have nothing.

Consider for a moment:

- Did you give yourself life? Did you create/design the way you look?
- Did you choose when you were born? Did you pick the family you were raised in?
- Did you give yourself your natural talents and abilities?
- Did you create the air you need to breathe?

I can keep going to prove the point.

- Did you design your brain with the ability to turn thoughts into ideas, to transform curiosity into creativity?
- How about the energy you need to make those creative ideas come to life? Do you have the ability to generate it for yourself, or do they require quality sleep, good food, and consistent exercise to become a reality?

My goal is not to ridicule us but to remind us of how generous God has been with us. James 1:17 says, "Every good and perfect gift is from above, coming down from the Father of the heavenly lights, who does not change like shifting shadows."

This should not make us feel small or insignificant but deeply loved. God has been so good to us. So how should we respond? Like good stewards, we should work hard and put the talents and abilities God has given us to good use serving others. This blesses them, brings us fulfillment, and honors God.

Every one of us should grow in our responsibility and become better stewards because those who are faithful with little will be given much.[4] We should want to grow into the best version of who God created us to be. God's not looking for a reason to give us less. But He always blesses us so we can *be* a blessing to others.

Three Ways to Be Generous

God wants us to have a generous spirit. He expects it. And as we'll learn, He gives us everything we need at all times to be generous in every occasion.

I think most people want to be generous, but they get stuck. The fear of not having enough is usually one of the driving forces. This fear doesn't just grip people who are living from paycheck to paycheck.

John D. Rockefeller founded Standard Oil and became one of the richest people in American history. One day a curious reporter asked him a fascinating question: "How much money does it take for a man to be happy?" Rockefeller's response has become legendary: "Just a little bit more."

Behind the fear is a desire for independent security. Human beings want to feel in control. The only problem is, we're not

---

[4] Matthew 25:23

in control. We never have been. Generosity comes from a heart that's surrendered to God as an acknowledgment that everything we have comes from Him. He's our source.

There are at least three ways for us to be generous.

① Our time

Most people are inclined to give where they have a surplus. Younger people tend to have more free time. As we get older, it can be easier to write a check than to make room on our calendars. On a daily basis, time is the one resource where we all get the same amount. Some people kill or waste time while others make or invest their time. How we use it demonstrates what matters to us.

② Our talent

Jesus challenged us to love others the way He loved us.[5] He told us He didn't come to be served but to serve others.[6] He said the greatest of all is the servant of all.[7] When we generously offer our talents as faithful stewards to bless others, we demonstrate our gratitude to our generous God.

"Each of you should use whatever gift you have received to serve others, as faithful stewards of God's grace in its various forms."[8]

③ Our treasure

Money is a great tool. It's useful. Used wisely it can make a massive impact. Some people think the Bible says money is "the

---

[5] John 13:34
[6] Matthew 20:28
[7] Matthew 23:11
[8] 1 Peter 4:10

root of all evil." It doesn't. It uses that phrase to describe the "love of money."[9]

But money is a terrible god. Money can't make you whole. Money can't tell you who you are. Money can't give you purpose or peace in your soul. Only God can do that.

Jesus said you can't serve two masters—you can't worship God *and* money (Luke 16:13). That's why God makes it easy for us to be generous with our treasure. He gives us a very clear plan to show we love Him more than we love money. Even the math is simple.

God wants to be first place in our hearts, not because He needs our money but because our hearts aren't whole when anything else comes before Him.

What Is the Tithe and Why Don't People Think It Applies to Them?

God has a plan for us to show we love Him more than money. He doesn't need our money. Our hearts need to be reminded He is our source. Everything we have comes from Him. We're not self-made.

To remind us and to help us grow in our generosity, God commands us to bring the first 10 percent of everything we make to Him. The Hebrew word for "tenth" is "tithe." Tithe is a church word. I don't think I've ever heard it used anywhere else, but it's not hard to understand. Ten percent is simple math—even a child can do it.

---

[9] 1 Timothy 6:10

It's bad grammar but it's had a big impact on my life: *I've never not tithed*. God's really smart. Like learning a foreign language, learning how to honor God with your tithe is much easier when you learn it as a small child. I'm so grateful for parents who taught me to tithe. It gets much more difficult as those numbers get bigger.

I realize there is a wide range of opinions on this subject and I've seen people manipulate the Bible in all kinds of ways to make it say what they want to. I'm fully aware there have been improper appeals from pastors and leaders. Typically, the motivation behind these actions is the fear that God won't provide.

This doesn't change the fact that Christians have lived this way for thousands of years, and in the process, they've provided significant enough resources to fund and fuel the mission of God in the earth through the Church.

Here are the two most common arguments I've heard against tithing:

① The tithe doesn't apply to us because it's an Old Testament idea. We're under the New Testament.

We can summarize this approach by equating tithing with other Old Testament laws, like dietary restrictions or detailed instructions on worship or clothing. We don't follow those anymore, so why would we follow the tithe? There are several problems with this line of thought.

First, Abraham and Jacob both tithed before God ever gave the Law to Moses. It was bigger than a rule. You could make a strong case that when Cain and Abel bring their offerings to God in

Genesis 4 they're giving their first 10 percent (the tithe). God gave Moses the Law to distinguish the people of God from everyone else in the earth.

> The tithe is not about religious protocol; it's a window into our hearts.

The second and bigger issue is that Jesus affirmed the tithe. In Matthew 23, there's a group of Pharisees who want everyone to see how righteous they are. They're taking the time to separate the first 10 percent of the spice they're putting on their food. Jesus could have said, "Guys, we don't do that anymore." But He didn't. He tells them to do it with the right motivation in their heart. That's the whole point—the tithe shows what's in your heart.

Think carefully if you're going to base your argument on the way Jesus applies the moral Old Testament principles to the people of His day. He exponentially raised the standard.

- He changed "an eye for an eye" to "love your enemies."
- He changed "don't murder" to "don't speak harshly to your enemies."
- He changed "don't commit adultery" to "don't have lustful thoughts."

If we apply this same approach to tithing, you're giving a lot more than 10 percent.

Followers of Christ in the New Testament lived with the expectation of generosity, especially toward those who gave themselves to the mission of preaching the gospel, serving churches, and advancing God's mission. If we take our lead from Jesus, tithing becomes a non-issue because it's always the floor—the bare minimum of what we do. Growth means we move to Spirit-led, cheerful giving far above and beyond 10 percent.

② The Church cares too much about money.

Stories of churches mismanaging resources tend to circulate. I get it. It's painful when someone abuses their influence, especially when it causes people to be mistreated. But if we can set this disappointment aside, we'd realize it's unrealistic to expect any meaningful organization to function without a budget or funding. No school, hospital, business, or family can be healthy without good stewardship.

No one stressed the importance of stewardship more than Jesus. If repetition equals emphasis, then He wanted to make sure we got the message. Almost half of His parables speak directly to the subject of handling money and possessions (16 out of 38).

A church is a reflection of the people who serve and lead it. If the church trusts God and honors Him with their resources, the church will be generous and a blessing to their city—through their giving and the attitude of their hearts, not just with their treasure but with their time and talent.

I'm so proud of the people of Milestone Church. It's an incredible privilege to serve one of the most generous churches in America. This is not a correction or an appeal to stir up giving. But it is important for you to understand how we live this value.

Biblical tithing assumes that God owns it all and you're only returning to Him what's already His. As individual stewards of our resources, we give to God and trust He directs it as He sees fit. This is not to imply the church bears no responsibility for how they use the resources entrusted to them. I don't believe this at all. Our entire team works very hard to be fiscally responsible and great stewards of what God has entrusted to us.

I hope these discussions have helped you think about tithing in a new light. I understand that well-meaning people with good intentions have questions. But I think the problem is deeper than that.

Three Reasons People Don't Tithe

My prayer is for you to hear my heart and to trust me when I say I want more for you than I want from you. I'm not giving you anything different than how I live myself or how I've talked about it with my kids. God makes it so practical because He wants us to see what's in our hearts. It's easy to hide around vague spiritual concepts. There's nuance and plenty of room for exceptions. The tithe is numbers. There's a right answer. It demonstrates our level of trust.

① They're afraid, and it's hard to start later in life.

I'm going to call it how it is: people from all over the world are moving to our region for economic opportunities. And despite economic ups and downs, we live in the most prosperous nation in the history of the world. Large amounts of money move in and out of our accounts, but when you start giving God your first 10 percent every month, the numbers are shocking.

When you learn to tithe as a child, the numbers are much smaller. Your faith grows and builds at each step. This is why I encourage parents to teach their children as early as possible.

I'm not surprised when people who've never heard of tithing look at me like I'm crazy. The lie is that this is easier for everyone else. It's not easy for anyone. Having more doesn't solve the problem—because the 10 percent is constant, the amount is a moving target. And that's why the tithe teaches you to trust God.

For years I've heard people say, "I can't afford to tithe!" I understand what they mean, but it doesn't make sense.

Everyone has a tithe—it's the first 10 percent no matter where it goes. Some people drive their tithe, some people live in their tithe, and others spend their weekends in the summer in their tithe.

② They think they're more generous than they are.
We all want to think of ourselves as generous but there may be no other value where the divide is so large between actual and aspirational. Most Christians give a tip—a little gratuity to God when they have a surplus—instead of the faithful, disciplined tithe.

③ They don't take God at His Word.
Intentions and feelings let us down. If we don't determine to obey God's Word, we'll always give ourselves a loophole. It's not uncommon for people to look at the tithe as something they can allocate to a favorite nonprofit, a humanitarian project, benevolence for a person in need, or educational expenses for their children. These can be good things, but they're not the tithe.

According to Leviticus 27:30 the tithe belongs to the Lord. Malachi 3:10 instructs us to bring the whole tithe into the storehouse—a representation of God's people, His family, His Church.

Paul told his son in the faith Timothy to command those who are rich in this present age not to be arrogant or to put their hope in wealth but to be rich in good deeds and to be generous.[10]

That command doesn't leave much room for personal preference, but I've never met anyone who thinks they're included in the "rich" category. All we need to give ourselves an out is to find someone who has more than us. That's not hard to do. But if we take the Bible seriously, we know He's talking to us.

God's not holding out on us. The same passage tells us He gives us everything for our enjoyment, and through our generosity we take hold of the life that is *really life*—the life we were created to live.

The more we trust God's Word, the more we realize generosity is like everything else God asks of us—not a way to give us less, but to experience more of His loving goodness.

We don't willpower our way into this kind of trust. When it comes to money, rules aren't enough to contain the unchecked desires of our hearts. How can we actually live this way?

Four Motivations Strong Enough to Make Us Generous

① We trust God as our source.

How confident is God in His ability to provide for us? Confident enough to do something crazy. There are very few places in the Bible where God tells us to test Him. In Malachi 3, God tells the people that because they don't trust Him, they've been stealing

---

[10] 1 Timothy 6:17-18

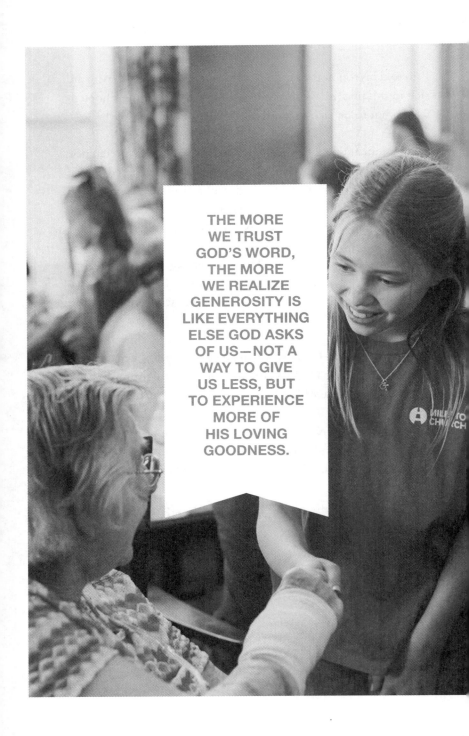

THE MORE WE TRUST GOD'S WORD, THE MORE WE REALIZE GENEROSITY IS LIKE EVERYTHING ELSE GOD ASKS OF US—NOT A WAY TO GIVE US LESS, BUT TO EXPERIENCE MORE OF HIS LOVING GOODNESS.

from Him. The people are defensive and they ask, "How have we been robbing you?"

His answer is short: *tithes and offerings*.

But God doesn't give up on them. He says, "Test me in this and see if I will not throw open the floodgates of heaven and pour out so much blessing that there will not be enough room to store it."[11] And when that happens, all the other nations will look at you and realize how much I've blessed you.

I love this about God. This passage is not a contract. It's much less about "Pay your tithes and God will give you money," and way more about "If you honor God with your hearts, you'll experience His presence and provision in such a powerful way that everyone else will look at you and see God's blessing in your life."

God's blessing is always about more than us. He blesses us to be a blessing. He's our provider, not our job, our salary, our investment portfolio, our next big deal, or the ups and downs of our economy.

Whatever we look to as our source takes the highest place in our hearts and our lives. If we genuinely believe God is our source, then we'll gladly put Him first. But if we look to something else to provide for us, we'll interpret God's love for us through our bank statement. I don't recommend this approach.

② We love God more than money.
This is the line in the sand Jesus drew for us. You can't love both. It's one or the other. This is the power of the firstfruits. Whatever we love most comes first.

[11] Malachi 3:10b

When Proverbs 3:9 tells us, "Honor the Lord with your wealth, with the firstfruits of all your crops," this is what it means. And let's be clear—it's all His anyway. It was never truly ours.

Most kids have thought about how they're going to spend money before they get it. Your teenager has a plan for that first paycheck. This is the same principle. When we can't wait to bring the first part to honor God, it demonstrates our love for Him in a powerful way.

③ We believe God has more, not less, for us.

One of the most common misunderstandings of God's generosity is to believe it's limited. If He gives to one person, it takes a piece of the pie that could have gone to someone else. The term for this is "zero-sum." There's only so much to go around. This causes us to have a scarcity mindset instead of an abundance mindset.

We may struggle to celebrate what God's doing for someone because deep down we're concerned that now we'll miss out. I can't tell you how damaging this is to your ongoing relationship with God. It keeps us from seeing Him for who He truly is—our loving, generous Father. He's generous with people who don't deserve it. He's an over-and-above God.

The further you drift from this picture of Him, the more distant you'll feel and the more isolated and disconnected you'll be—in ways that have far more unintended outcomes than just your budget. You don't want to live this way. It's miserable. It's so much less than what He has for us.

God is always looking for opportunities to be generous. And generous people live like Him. They're always ready to give. In 2

Corinthians 9:10–11, Paul describes God as the one who supplies both seed to the sower *and* bread for food. Think about that. You eat bread; you sow seed. Both come from God.

In other words, God has a reserve of resources only available to those generous enough to always be ready to invest and sow seed. The seed is not for the hungry or the needy. He cares about them and meets their needs, but He gives seed to sowers.

Seeds take time. They have to be sown in advance. Seed that goes in the ground becomes wheat that's milled, turned into grain, and baked to make bread. That bread meets an immediate need, but generous people never stop sowing seed. They're not worried about a scarcity of bread; they're sowing an abundance of seed because they believe God has more for them.

> God has a reserve of resources only available to those generous enough to always be ready to invest and sow seed.

④ **We believe God's plan begins with His Church.**
We know how much God values His Church. He loves it as His people, His family, His body, and His bride. His Church is the only thing Jesus promised to build. When you see the Church the way Jesus does, giving is not an obligation; it's a privilege. It's the best investment we can make.

God wants us to be like Him. The more we become like Him, the more we care about what He cares about. He cares about people. He cares about His Church. He cares about us. And we have the confidence that He always enriches us in every way so we can be generous on every occasion.

KEY THOUGHTS

- Generosity is not money. Money is a resource; generosity is an attitude toward life. God wants us to be generous, because we're made in His image.

- *Everything* belongs to God. We're not owners; we're all stewards—managers of what we've been entrusted with.

- Three ways to be generous:
    1. Our time
    2. Our talent
    3. Our treasure

    When we generously offer our time, talents, and treasure as faithful stewards to bless others, we demonstrate our gratitude to our generous God.

- What is a tithe? The Hebrew word for "tenth" is "tithe." To remind us and to help us grow in our generosity, God commands us to bring the first 10 percent of everything we make to Him.

- Why don't people think tithing applies to them?
    1. They think it's an Old Testament idea.
    2. They think that the Church cares too much about money.

- God wants to be first place in our hearts, not because He needs our money, but because our hearts aren't whole when anything else comes before Him.

- Three reasons people don't tithe:
    1. They're afraid, and it's hard to start later in life.
    2. They think they're more generous than they are.
    3. They don't take God at His Word.

- Generosity is like everything else God asks of us—not a way to give us less, but a way to experience more of Him.

- Four motivations strong enough to make us generous:
    1. We trust God as our source.
    2. We love God more than money.
    3. We believe God has more, not less, for us.
    4. We believe God's plan begins with His Church.

NEXT STEPS

—The first step in generosity always starts with firstfruits and the tithe. Set aside the first 10 percent of your income and give it straight to the church God has placed you in. In addition to your tithe, give generously through offerings.

—Next, give where it hurts the most. Contemplate the resource that is most difficult for you to give and make it a practice to prioritize this kind of giving.

11

HOW DOES
THE HOLY SPIRIT
HELP US?

THE TRINITY IS ONE OF THE most important concepts in the entire Bible—there is one God eternally existent in three persons: the Father, the Son, and the Holy Spirit.

Some aspects of this are easier for us to grasp than others. Most people understand the idea of God as Father. And Jesus as the Son of God helps to make this concept real in every culture of the world. Through His life, His example, and His words, Jesus shows us who God is.

So far so good. But what about the other guy? I've found a majority of people aren't sure what to do with Him.

Maybe it's because they've heard Him described as "the Holy Ghost." What are we supposed to do with that?

Maybe they've seen some eccentric expressions or behaviors

IT'S WORTH IT 2.0

attributed to the Holy Spirit, and it made them feel a little weird. Maybe they come from a faith tradition that doesn't have a theological box to put Him in. Or maybe no one ever really talked about Him.

Wherever you are and however you got there, my goal for all of us is the same: *I'm praying we'll grow in our relationship with the Holy Spirit because He can help us like no one else can.*

In order for us to grow in our relationship with Him, we need to understand who He is—and who He isn't.

Who Is the Holy Spirit?

The Holy Spirit is not a style of worship.

Over the past few decades, it's become common for people to describe a church as "Spirit-filled." They may even ask me, "Is your church one of those Holy Ghost churches?" I'm not exactly sure what they mean when they ask this, but I have an idea. They're trying to imagine the environment and our expression of worship. What's it like in there? Is it more traditional with pews and an organ, or is there a band with people moving and lifting their hands?

Different people appreciate different styles of worship. The Holy Spirit can and does move through them all. That's not the issue.

The Holy Spirit is not a cloud, a vapor, or a feeling.

This is a big one. In the Western world, we struggle with things of the Spirit. We lean toward skepticism. We tend to prioritize things we can prove over things we can perceive. When we can't fully make sense of something, we minimize it.

198 CHAPTER 11 I HOW DOES THE HOLY SPIRIT HELP US?

The Holy Spirit is not a license to be weird or spontaneous and overly spiritual.

Well-meaning people have occasionally and perhaps unintentionally given Him a bad reputation. In their excitement and zeal, they emphasized their personality more than His person.

The Holy Spirit is a person.

Hopefully you noticed I've never described Him as an "it." This is 100 percent on purpose. He's never been an "it." He's not an object; He's a person. You can have a relationship with Him. In fact, He's always with the believer because He makes His home in us.

The Holy Spirit is fully God.

He doesn't show up near the end of the Bible after Jesus ascends to heaven. The Holy Spirit is present and active throughout the entire Bible. He was present at creation. He moved through the earth in Noah's days. He was so active in Joseph's life that Pharaoh sees the Spirit in him. And that's just the book of Genesis. He moved through kings, came upon prophets, and touched the lives of ordinary people.

With this new understanding of the relational and personal nature of the Holy Spirit, it would help us to understand why God sent Him. No one understood this better than Jesus. During their time with Him, the disciples saw the Spirit on Him and working through Him on a daily basis.

As we've seen, when Jesus went to Jerusalem for the Passion week leading up to Easter, He was preparing them to carry on His Great Commission. In order to get them ready, He gave them the lengthiest and most detailed teaching on the Holy Spirit.

How Did Jesus Help His Disciples Relate to the Holy Spirit?

Imagine you're one of the disciples. You think you're going to Jerusalem to celebrate the Passover like you did every year. Only this time it's completely different. After occasionally hinting at this idea, Jesus has told you He's going to be betrayed, arrested, and crucified.

It's going to happen.

Think how devastated you would be. You'd be freaking out. You gave up everything—your business, your whole life—to follow Him, and now He was leaving. You'd be tempted to think it was all for nothing. Instead, Jesus tells you not to worry because He would send you the Helper, the Holy Spirit, to be with you.

In John 16:7 (NASB), Jesus tells them it's to their "advantage" that He goes away. This is crazy! How could it possibly be better to be without Him? Jesus goes on to tell them He has many more things to say to them but they can't handle it. But the Holy Spirit would lead them and guide them into all truth. He'd help them make sense of their world that was about to be turned upside down.

After Jesus is crucified and the disciples find out the tomb is empty, they're all scared of the Jewish leaders and hide in a room behind a locked door. All of a sudden, Jesus shows up and gives them His peace. In John 20:22, He breathes on them and says, "Receive the Holy Spirit."

If that seems weird, the Hebrew word for "spirit" (*ruach*) is the same word for "breath." This is why Genesis 2:7 tells us God breathed into man and he became a living being. Initially God breathed His Spirit into man to give him life. Now He's doing it again to give them new life.

Most Bible scholars believe this is the moment of salvation for the disciples. However we make sense of that, if the resurrected Jesus gives them the Holy Spirit, it's safe to say they now have Him living inside of them.

In Luke's version of this same story, in 24:49, Jesus tells them He's going to send them what the Father had promised, but He instructs them to stay and wait in the city until they're clothed with power from on high.

I like to think of it this way: Jesus was saying, "You're going to go and preach the gospel to all the nations. But don't do *anything* until you've got the power."

The story picks up in Acts 1:8 (Luke wrote both the Gospel of Luke and Acts—it's like the sequel) when the disciples remember Jesus told them to wait in the city for the power. This power would come when the Holy Spirit came upon them, and He would give them power to be His witnesses.

They'd already received the Holy Spirit on the night of Easter Sunday when He showed up and breathed on them. Now they were being filled again. Acts 2:4 tells us that on the day of Pentecost, all of them were filled with the Spirit. This was about more than a worship expression (although that happened too). This was more than an obscure teaching.

Later that day Peter preaches his first message, and he's not the same person. He's bold. He's direct. His words have the power of the Holy Spirit on them. When He finishes, the people ask, "What must we do to be saved?" Thousands of people give their lives to Christ.

At the end of his message in verses 38 and 39, Peter promises that the people who believe will receive the gift of the Holy Spirit. He says this gift is available for them, for their children, for those who are far off, and for all whom the Lord will call.

In case you're wondering, we're included in that "all." This gift of the Holy Spirit, this power to be a witness, is available for us.

WHEN THE HOLY SPIRIT IS MOVING, THERE'S POWER TO BE A WITNESS, THERE'S THE BOLD PROCLAMATION OF THE WORD, AND THERE ARE PEOPLE COMING INTO A RELATIONSHIP WITH JESUS.

Peter and John and the disciples keep preaching; they pray for sick people and see them healed—they basically turn the city upside down. The religious leaders are so angry that they call them in, command them to stop, threaten them, and throw them in jail. But Peter and John basically say, "Do what you gotta do, but we're not stopping."

The religious leaders don't know what to do next, so Peter and John go meet up with the other disciples and tell them what happened. They start praying, and Acts 4:31 tells us they're all filled with the Holy Spirit again and they speak the word of God boldly.

This pattern didn't stop with the disciples. It's passed throughout the early church. By the middle of the book of Acts, Paul has experienced this himself and trained those he led to depend on the power of the Holy Spirit too.

In Ephesians 5:18b, he gives a simple and clear bottom line for how believers should relate to the Holy Spirit: "be filled." The verb tense for filled is ongoing. In other words, it's probably closer to say, "Keep being filled."

If we summarize how Jesus led the disciples to relate to the Holy Spirit, we see a pattern of prayer, power, continual filling, and a boldness to speak the Word. That's what He trained them to expect.

Based on this progression and the way Jesus set it up, when a person says, "The Holy Spirit is really moving in that church," I don't expect that to mean there was a deep, obscure Bible teaching or an unusual expression of worship. Somehow this has become normal in certain circles, but it's not consistent with the big story of Scripture.

When the Holy Spirit is moving, there's power to be a witness, there's the bold proclamation of the Word, and there are people coming into a relationship with Jesus.

It seems so clear. So why don't we hear more about Him? Why don't more people have a dynamic relationship with Him?

Two Points of Contention

Unfortunately, there's apprehension around the subject—enough to cause people to ask questions like, "Do I have to be filled with the Spirit to be a follower of Christ?" That's kind of like asking, "If I'm on the team, do I have to go in the game?"

No. But why wouldn't you want to? I've found there are two primary points of contention that keep people from moving forward.

My goal is to help you understand why there's reluctance, not to perpetuate an argument. My heart for you is that God will continue to guide you through the process.

① Is there a subsequent work of the Holy Spirit?

This objection is typically motivated by feeling slighted. Under-standably, believers object to the idea that the initial work of the Holy Spirit is insufficient. This is not what we're saying at all. The Bible is clear: the Holy Spirit comes and lives inside you at the moment of salvation.

Let's go back to our helpful distinction between justification and sanctification. Justification happens in a moment. We can't earn it. We receive it as a gift from God. While we are enemies, while we are separated from God, He gives His Son to die on our behalf and Jesus exchanges His perfect righteousness for our sin. In that moment we can now have peace with God, we're adopted into His family, and we're sealed with the Holy Spirit who comes and lives inside of us. Nothing needs to be added for us to be right with God.[1]

---

[1] Ephesians 1:13-14

However, there is a process of sanctification. It doesn't make us right with God—justification accomplishes that. But sanctification is the process where we become more and more like Him. This is the process of discipleship, where one Christ-follower helps another take their next step. It's how we grow. It's how we become more and more of who God created us to be.

And one of the primary catalysts of this process is the ongoing and empowering work of the Holy Spirit. It does not make us more saved, or make God love us more, but it does build our character and help us enjoy our lives at a deeper level.

You might be thinking, *Jeff, is that what it means to be filled with the Spirit? Is that what it means to be baptized in the Holy Spirit?* I think it's less about terms and labels and more about a heart that's open to God.

② Does God still work through the gifts of the Spirit and perform miracles?

All Christians believe God gave gifts and performed miracles through the apostles to build and establish the Church as we clearly see throughout the book of Acts and the New Testament. Some churches believe this was a temporary approach until the Bible was completed and then the gifts stopped.

The explanation for this perspective is a particular reading of 1 Corinthians 13:8-10 (ESV) that lists a variety of spiritual gifts before stating this phrase: "when the perfect comes, the partial will pass away." This group interprets "the perfect" as the delivery of the Bible in its final form. Once we get the finished Word of God, we no longer need the gifts. I agree the Bible is perfect, but I do not believe that's what this passage means. The reason I think this is that verse 12 of the same chapter says that when the perfect has come, we'll know fully, even as we're fully known.

I love the Bible. I can't live without it. But I can't say that reading the Bible has allowed me to know Jesus as fully as He knows me. This line of reasoning breaks down. I believe, like 1 John 3:2, that this passage is referring to when Jesus returns and we receive our glorified, resurrected bodies. On that day, we'll see Him and know Him in all His fullness.

Other churches believe God gave these gifts to all believers and they continue to be in use for the common good and to advance the mission of the Church. They also believe in the ongoing and empowering presence of the Holy Spirit in the life of the believer.

In other words, with very few exceptions, people either say yes or no to both of these contentions.

We believe, with the rest of Christian history, that well–meaning followers of Christ can come to different conclusions about these two questions while maintaining a healthy relationship with Jesus and with each other.

Like many people I've met throughout my years of ministry, I grew up in an environment where we firmly said no to both of these. While I'm grateful for my heritage and their love for the Word, I've come to the conviction that the overwhelming perspective of the Bible says yes to both questions.

I can appreciate firsthand the difficulty of navigating some of the challenges of honoring our family and our faith traditions while also continuing to grow and develop our own convictions about these important issues. If this is an issue you're wrestling with, I want you to understand that my desire is not to persuade you or solve it, but to help you as you continue to pray and grow in this aspect of your relationship with God.

If all of this is new to you and you're just now forming your belief system, this may help you. While I respect and give room for every believer to form their own conviction, there is no doubt in my mind that people who believe in the active and present work of the Holy Spirit live differently.

This does not mean they have fewer problems or challenges. In most cases they have more. But they also receive supernatural help and power for those challenges simply because they're open to receiving it.

Active   Present Holy Spirit   Help   Power

They're not a higher level of Christian or more loved by God, but a big part of receiving help from God is asking for it and expecting to receive it.

How Does the Holy Spirit Help Us?

You're probably wondering, *Jeff, if we believe He's active and present in our lives, and we can expect His help and His power, how does that actually work?* Great question. I want to make it as practical as possible.

① He guides us.

Jesus said the Holy Spirit would lead us and guide us into all truth. He gives wise counsel, speaks to us in prayerful decisions, and provides input on anything we ask Him about. If you're wondering how we can tell it's the Holy Spirit speaking to us, we always have the assurance that He'll never say anything that contradicts God's Word.

Does this guidance line up with Scripture? Does it reinforce what we know to be true? Does it build our faith and make God bigger in our eyes? These are all great indicators we're being guided by the Spirit.

Jesus called Him our "Advocate," which is another term for "lawyer." The primary context is a defense attorney—He stands with us and pleads our case when we're being accused by the enemy. So much of the confusion and resistance we face in this world is not the result of our boss, our difficult family members, a politician, or any other human being. These are spiritual forces. The Holy Spirit gives us spiritual means to resist the strategies of the enemy. And He also gives us the confidence to remember that in Jesus, every victory has already been won.

We don't fight to get the victory; we fight *from* the victory Jesus won through triumphing over sin, death, hell, and the grave. The Holy Spirit reminds us of this powerful truth, especially when the enemy comes to accuse us.

Another role of an advocate, a helper, is legal counsel. There is no human counselor like Him.

② He reminds us of the truth.

Jesus said one of the primary roles of the Holy Spirit is to remind us of everything Jesus said. Maybe you're not the kind of person who likes to read. Maybe you have a hard time remembering the reason you went into the kitchen, much less a chapter and verse from the Bible! This is where the Holy Spirit comes in.

As you grow in your relationship with Him, He nudges you; He brings things to the screen of your mind; He gives you the ability outside of your own talent to recall the words of Jesus. Sometimes He speaks directly. Sometimes He directs a friend to send you a text. However He does it, you can be certain the more time you spend with the Holy Spirit, the more you'll be directed back to the Word.

③ He provides real help in all of our weaknesses.

The disciples were keenly aware of their weaknesses. Not only were they scared of what others would think, they were also beaten and thrown in jail. They couldn't rely on their training, their influence, or

JESUS SAID THE HOLY SPIRIT WOULD LEAD US AND GUIDE US INTO ALL TRUTH.

their natural powers of persuasion. They needed supernatural power—and they got it every time.

The same Holy Spirit who moved through them is at work in us. He provides power, comfort, guidance, strength, and encouragement, and He gives us good gifts. As we use these gifts to serve others, our relationship with the Holy Spirit continues to grow.

One of the ways the Spirit helps us in our weakness is when we don't know how to pray. "In the same way the Spirit also helps our weakness; for we don't know how to pray as we should, but the Spirit himself intercedes for us with groanings too deep for words."[2]

Sometimes praying in the Spirit means the Holy Spirit guides us and coaches us in topics that He wants us to cover. But it also means sometimes we don't know what to pray, and the Holy Spirit prays through us in a language we don't naturally speak.

Again, let's not make this a false dichotomy. We're not pitting praying with our own words against praying in the Spirit through words we don't understand. No, you do not have to do this. But if you want to, it's available to you. God generously gives us the ability to pray both ways because He loves us and He wants to help us.

You might be thinking, *Is that somewhere else in the Bible?* In Paul's letter to the church in Corinth, he's talking about how to use the gifts in a sensible way that doesn't become a distraction and helps everyone grow closer to God.[3] Toward the end of the discussion, Paul sums up his attitude toward this subject: "What is

---

[2] Romans 8:26, NASB
[3] 1 Corinthians 1:7; 3:1

the outcome then? I will pray with the spirit and I will pray with the mind also."[4]

How Do We Relate to the Holy Spirit?

As we come to a close, remember where we started. My prayer for all of us was to grow in our relationship with the Holy Spirit. He lives inside of us. He has the power to help us. But what does He expect of us? And how can we strengthen our relationship with Him?

① We don't grieve Him; we honor Him.

Ephesians 4:30 challenges us not to grieve the Holy Spirit. This comes out of a larger discussion about watching how we talk and getting rid of bad attitudes and habits, like bitterness, anger, slander, and malice.

Because He's a person, we can offend Him. We can make Him sad or disappointed. Like us, He tends to move away from environments where things are present that He does not enjoy. And He moves toward places where He's honored and the things of God are celebrated.

I don't know exactly how all these specifics work, but I want to be the kind of person who makes Him feel welcome. It's a relationship we cultivate, just like any other.

② We prioritize the fruit of the Spirit over the gifts of the Spirit.

There can be a faulty perception that the gifts of the Spirit are so powerful that we should put up with potential baggage that

---

[4] 1 Corinthians 14:15a, NASB

may come with them. This is what happened in the church at Corinth. They tolerated the issues of gifted people because they wanted their gift. This is a human response, not a biblical one.

Because the Holy Spirit is fully God, He's always thinking about people—especially people who are far from Him. This is why He doesn't act in a way to repel or confuse those who don't know or understand Him.

The fruit of the Spirit (love, joy, peace, forbearance, kindness, goodness, faithfulness, gentleness, and self-control [see Galatians 5:22]) always communicates God's character. The gifts of the Spirit often communicate His power. Because God is so generous, He gives His gifts freely—even though they're not always used in the right way. We're all growing and learning, so we want to give plenty of room and opportunity for people to grow and receive coaching in using their gifts, but never at the expense of loving others.

It's the fruit of the Spirit, not the gifts of the Spirit, that demonstrate the maturity of the believer.

③ We spend time with Him, ask Him to fill us, and ask Him for His gifts.

The best way I can summarize how we should relate to the Holy Spirit is to simply *be with Him*. Invite Him into our day-to-day lives. Ask Him for help at work. Invite Him to give insight into our spouses. Ask Him to give us grace and favor for the difficult conversations we're having with our teenagers.

You might be wondering, *Is that allowed, Jeff? He's gotta be busy. Is it okay for me to bring those kinds of things to Him?* In Luke 11:13,

IT'S THE FRUIT OF THE SPIRIT, NOT THE GIFTS OF THE SPIRIT, THAT DEMONSTRATE THE MATURITY OF THE BELIEVER.

Jesus said that even though human dads have struggles, they still do their best to give gifts to their children. If that's true, how much more will our perfect Father give the Holy Spirit to those who ask for Him! He wants us to ask. He's ready and waiting.

Remember, when Paul tells the church in Ephesus to be filled with the Spirit (see Ephesians 5:18-20), the verb tense for "filled" is ongoing. It's not a one-time thing. He goes on to say speak to each other with psalms, sing in the Spirit, always giving thanks to the Father. These are more than activities—they're a lifestyle. It's a posture Paul wants us to have before God because the Spirit fills people who live this way.

What a great goal for all of us.

KEY THOUGHTS

- The Holy Spirit is not a style of worship or a feeling. The Holy Spirit is a person you can have a relationship with. He is fully God, present and active throughout the entire Bible.

- The Holy Spirit is God's gift to us. If we summarize how Jesus led the disciples to relate to the Holy Spirit, we see a pattern of prayer, power, continual filling, and a boldness to speak the Word.

- Two points of contention on the Holy Spirit:
    1. Is there a subsequent work of the Holy Spirit?
    2. Does God still work through the gifts of the Spirit and perform miracles?

    The overwhelming perspective of the Bible says yes to both questions.

- People who believe in the active and present work of the Holy Spirit live differently.

- How does the Holy Spirit help us?
    1. He guides us.
    2. He reminds us of the truth.
    3. He provides real help in all of our weaknesses.

- One of the ways the Spirit helps us in our weakness is when we don't know how to pray. God generously gives us the ability to pray with our minds and our spirits because He loves us and He wants to help us.

- How do we relate to the Holy Spirit?

    1. We don't grieve Him; we honor Him.

    2. We prioritize the fruit of the Spirit over the gifts of the Spirit.

    3. We spend time with Him, ask Him to fill us, and ask Him for His gifts.

- We learn to relate to the Holy Spirit when we're *with Him*. Invite Him into your day-to-day life.

NEXT STEPS ✓

—If you've never done it, read through the progression of how Jesus helped the disciples, referenced on p. 200.

—When was the last time you asked the Holy Spirit to fill you? Based on the promise in Luke 11:13, all you have to do is ask!

SECTION 03

SECTION 03

WHERE ARE WE GOING?

12

GROWTH AND EXPANSION

STOP FOR A MOMENT AND THINK about the future. Imagine you're looking out over the next 10, 15, 20 years. What would you like to see?

For most of us, we think about the hopes and dreams we have for our immediate family. I'm with you. I have all kinds of things I'm praying for my kids. I'm trying to get them off the payroll and I'm hoping for a whole bunch of grandkids. Brandy and I still have plenty we're asking God to do in our lives. There's no shortage of vision for our family.

But what if we stretch it out a little further? What about our friends, our neighbors, our co-workers, and the thousands of people moving to the Dallas/Fort Worth area? What do we want for them? What if we looked beyond that to the extended region and even across our country?

I'm guessing you want for them what's been meaningful to you. You want them to experience the goodness and grace of God you've received. Me too.

How are we going to make this happen? Let me be clear: I realize it's not all on us. But we do have a stewardship. We have a part to play. God has given us the opportunity to make an impact in this moment in time. So how do we do that?

Here's the way I believe God has asked us to do our part: *one church in multiple locations.*

It may be hard to get your mind around, but there are lots of things that grow and develop over time. Has your concept of the phone changed over the past 15 years? I know mine has.

I remember the first time someone tried to explain an SMS to me. I had no clue what they were talking about. Today we all send way more texts on our phones than we do anything else.

I realize this phrase—"one church in multiple locations"—may sound crazy to you, but I'm hoping over the next few years it will become normal. Why is it so important?

Because I believe it's the strategy God has given us to continue to expand what He has done in and through us. It's not a theory; it's already happening.

One church in multiple locations allows God to reach more people and build more lives. It allows more people to use their gifts and more space to open up for guests and loved ones who are far from God. It allows more young leaders to be called into the mission, experience the joy of advancing God's Kingdom, and realize their destiny.

But one church in multiple locations will cause us to make some changes too.

It means we can't hold on to what we have right now with a closed fist. We may need to attend a different service. Our Small Groups won't be together until Jesus returns. The people we see every week on the Serve Team won't stay the same.

I realize this can be difficult for the majority of people—because we don't like change. But everything that's healthy grows, and there's no growth without change. This requires us to adjust our thinking. Instead of focusing on what we're losing, we have to think about all that God is adding to our lives.

Remember, Milestone Church is a family. And in every healthy family, everyone grows, and this means life continues to change. We named it Milestone Church because we wanted to be intentional about celebrating what God is doing at every step along the way—and we're more committed to this than ever.

This also means we have to keep our hearts open and ready for change. I'm not correcting you—you're doing so great at this. It's one of the many reasons I'm so grateful to be your pastor. But we all need a healthy reminder every once in a while.

Our hearts need to be ready for the changes God may ask us to make.

And in one church with multiple locations, change could even mean leaving your current campus to join a new one closer to your home. Like any other change, these moments come with both positives and negatives.

The good news: a much shorter drive time, great opportunities to serve/lead, and a new incentive to invite friends and co-workers to church. The bad news: you'll see some of your church family less, and you'll have to adjust to some new worship leaders, and service hosts. But we've found that for many people, over time, some of the things they thought would be a negative jumped over to the positive as they grew to appreciate it.

I understand how perceptions of larger churches can be a powerful influence. You're worried they become impersonal and treat you like a number. The pastor changes and the church gets weird.

But what if we're thinking about it wrong? I like to say big churches can solve big problems. No one has a problem when a big church has the ability to deploy thousands of people into the surrounding area to serve and care for people.

What if a big church can actually become *more* loving? The Bible thinks it's possible.

One Church in Multiple Locations Allows More People to Use Their Gifts

The book of Ephesians is Paul's letter to the church at Ephesus. It was a large church in a trade city where lots of people moved for economic opportunities. Paul's son in the faith, Timothy, was the pastor. Scholars believe that for a period of time the apostle John was a member of the church and served the people there.

In Ephesians 4, Paul encourages them to become more of who God created them to be. He explains that God has called a few people to a life of vocational ministry as pastors and leaders in the church. They're more than professional Christians. Their job is not to do all the ministry when the church gathers but to equip all the people in the church to serve and minister to each other. Under the inspiration of the Holy Spirit, Paul says this is the key to building up the church in faith and causing it to grow to maturity.

A church where all the people do ministry is a mature church. That kind of church speaks the truth in love and grows to look more and more like Jesus—the head of the body. And then Paul makes an incredible statement in verse 16:

> From him the whole body, joined and held together
> by every supporting ligament, grows and builds itself
> up in love, as each part does its work.

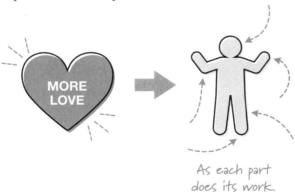

As each part
does its work.

I love this. When every person in a church engages with the mission of God and uses their gifts to serve people, the church builds itself up in love. What does our broken and hurting world need? More love! New campuses create new opportunities for more people to do their part. At a new campus, the need for each person to jump in and offer their gifts is immediately clear. No one can do everything, but everyone can do something.

Size has nothing to do with how loving an environment can be.

I think deep down we know this. It's the health and values of the culture, not the size, that determine how loving it is. This is true whether we're talking about families, businesses, or certainly churches.

There are small families that are cold and unloving. There are big families where new cousins and distant relatives may not even know each other's names but the entire gathering is so filled with love that in no time people grow close.

I believe the same is true of churches. There are small churches where people know your name and they know who you are. That's not the issue. The problem is, the church isn't welcoming or loving.

WHEN EVERY PERSON IN A CHURCH ENGAGES WITH THE MISSION OF GOD AND USES THEIR GIFTS TO SERVE PEOPLE, THE CHURCH BUILDS ITSELF UP IN LOVE.

And whether you're a big church or a small church, you're still dealing with imperfect people. This means there will be plenty of opportunities to be offended and plenty of opportunities to ask for and extend forgiveness. But as we discussed in chapter 9, when we believe God has placed us in the body right where He wants us, we predetermine to extend grace and forgiveness even when we don't feel like it.

One church in multiple locations helps keep a bigger church feeling smaller. The truth is, sociologists suggest you can really only maintain relationships with 150 people. Often the people who struggle with the church getting "too big" are really reacting to the feeling that they don't know what's happening with everyone. This grates on their sense of security and confidence because it's easy to feel overlooked or left out.

But the truth is, we can't really keep up with what's happening with everyone. And the good news is, God hasn't asked us to. It's hard to feel overlooked or left out when you're spending the majority of your time thinking about how you can serve the new people God is bringing. This makes them feel loved and brings you fulfillment.

We Start with a Growth Plan

You're probably wondering, *Okay, Jeff. I get it. In order to reach more people, the church has to expand. How do we know where to go? Or better yet, how can we get a Milestone Church close to people I care about?!*

I love this question! This is what I want you to ask—and no, I didn't make it up for the sake of this book. I get asked this question all the time and it makes me feel so proud of you because it shows you want the people you love to experience what God has done in you.

That's the whole purpose of why we want to expand.

We have big vision and big dreams because we serve a big God. We would love to cover as much ground and reach as many people for Jesus as we possibly can. We're trying to follow the expansion model in the book of Acts. How do we strategically spread out and reach important centers in our region?

We would love to expand to as many places as possible, but we're trying our best to be wise stewards and to ensure our ability to care for people in sustainable ways. So we do our due diligence to evaluate our next moves.

We Wrestle with Strategic Questions

In the process of growth and expansion, we move from a general growth plan to wrestling with strategic questions. I've listed a few of the most common questions people ask when we talk about this subject together.

Question: How do you know where to start a campus?

Like everything else we do, we start with the concept of stewardship from God. We don't start with what we feel like doing. Who has God entrusted to us? We look at the demographics for our current campuses, especially our Keller campus. Where are people coming from? Are there pockets of people who are driving an extended distance to be part of what we're doing? How could we serve them better?

But that's only one aspect. We also have to consider whether we have the right leaders in place, what kind of available meeting space we can find, whether there are opportunities to purchase land, and if God is calling us there.

We trust that God will open the right doors at the right time. We believe there will be many new campuses in the coming years, and we want to do our absolute best to give every one of those campuses the opportunity to be effective in the mission of reaching people and building lives.

We have big vision and big dreams because we serve a big God.

Question: Why do you use video in your services?

What I've learned over the years is, the message takes priority over the medium. If the message communicates God's Word in a powerful way that leads to growth and change, the way it comes to us is not as important. We're also going to continue to develop communicators who use their gifts to love and serve people—just like we do in all of the other areas of our church family.

We also use video for the same reasons we have multiple services and multiple locations: we feel it's the best way for us to love and serve people. The only people who like services that are overflowing are staff and volunteers. We like it because it means more people are being reached. But studies have shown that when someone new comes into an environment, if the worship center is 80 percent full, it feels too crowded.

More services give us a greater opportunity to reach more people, but it also creates a new challenge.

You probably don't realize this, but experts have suggested that preaching one message in one service requires the same emotional energy as a typical 8-hour work day. Now imagine repeating that 8-hour work day two times every Saturday followed by three times on Sunday—and then doing that 35 to 40 times per year. I'm grateful our board won't allow me to do it. I care about people and I want to give them the best experience, so I'm tempted at times to do it anyway.

However, we've found that after a few minutes, the average person forgets they're watching a video rather than listening to a person standing in front of them. Our production team does a phenomenal job keeping everything running smoothly and continuing to help our communicators to look in the camera and to speak to the different audiences who are following along.

Another reason we use videos at our campuses is the time and freedom it gives the campus pastor to concentrate on other tasks. The staff team at our Keller campus is larger and can accommodate more of the weekly weight it requires to pull off weekend services. This allows the majority of resources at our campuses to be directed to connecting with and reaching new people.

All of our campuses have live worship, live hosting from a campus pastor, and then a message. All campuses play a video in some services. Periodically throughout the year, most campuses will have a live communicator. Whether in person or through video, our heart remains the same. We're trusting that God will move through the communicator to impact the lives of people. That's why we do it—to love and serve people.

Question: How do people at different campuses relate to each other?

The whole purpose behind one church in multiple locations is to reinforce the concept of spiritual family. We're a family, a body, a team God has placed together for the expressed purpose of reaching people and building lives.

Every location has weekend services and the Growth Track. Every location lives out our five values. Every location is filled with volunteers who serve and love others in order to reach people and build lives. And every location offers every person the opportunity to take their next step.

When church members from different campuses meet each other, they treat each other like family. They look for ways to love and serve each other, not to compete with or criticize each other.

Church members at different campuses aren't selective on who they trust or honor. There's not a hierarchy or a system of preference. From our heart we say, "That's my church. That's my pastor." As one church with a growing number of locations, the expression at each campus may be slightly different, but the heart remains the same.

We'll always do our best to give every location the opportunity to experience everything God has for them, but it's not possible to scale all the same events to all the same locations. Because we're one church family, in those situations, members from other locations are always welcome to come over and participate.

This is the kind of church we want to be. We're an everyone church, where every person is made in the image of God and has something to offer. We believe there's a spot on the team for them and there's a unique contribution God has given them

Question: What about church online? How does that work?

Our online church has two primary functions:

1. To provide a first impression for all people learning more about Milestone Church
2. To serve as the campus for people who don't live near one of our physical campuses

Here's what we realized: Before most people step foot on one of our physical locations, they will experience us online. Nearly every person who comes to visit us has looked at our website and watched part of a service—especially the message.

This makes perfect sense. Don't you do the same thing before you go to a new restaurant, hotel, or concert venue? You're trying to get a sense of what your experience will be like. I do the same thing.

In other words, more people will interact with Milestone Church for the first time through a screen than through a person.

For the majority of the history of Milestone Church, when we asked someone who was visiting for the first time how they got here, the most common response was "My friend invited me." A few years ago, our staff discovered this was no longer the top answer. For at least the past five years (or more), it's been replaced by "We found you online."

I'm not suggesting we put any less energy into serving people well, but I am suggesting our reach has changed. We have to continue to get better in meeting people's needs through our digital platforms.

Some consultants and prognosticators have suggested the online experience will replace physical gatherings. Let me be clear: I don't believe this is true. If the pandemic has taught us anything, it's that the majority of people need more than what a Zoom gathering can provide; we need to be with people.

But I also don't believe these two environments have to compete with each other. I believe there are incredible opportunities for them to strengthen the effectiveness and impact each unique experience provides.

I believe it's possible for people to genuinely experience spiritual family through an online campus. Our team has not solved all the challenges we'll encounter, but we're committed to getting there.

By this point, I hope you realize that's the same goal at each of our physical locations. In both settings the goal is the same:

reaching people and building lives. Same vision, different campus. We want to see one Christ-follower help another Christ-follower take their next step.

This is more than an aspirational goal; it's already happening. At the time of writing this, through our online campus over the last few weeks, 21 people have texted for prayer or input. We've had four people give their lives to Christ. We've had people plan their visit to a physical location after participating in an online service.

It's happening.

For years, people from our physical locations have delivered welcome baskets to new people who've moved to the area as a way to say, "We're glad you're here and we would love the opportunity to serve you." We want people who come to our online church to experience this same loving kindness and warmth.

Camryn and Lance

Camryn and Lance graduated from Baylor University and were moving to the area for a new job. One of Camryn's sorority sisters was from Keller and told her about Milestone. They decided to watch online for a couple weeks before the move. By the time they arrived in Keller, they already felt like they were part of the family. They immediately jumped into the Growth Track, made good friends, and found places to serve and use their gifts.

This is how spiritual family works.

> ## Andy
>
> "I have been a member of the Online Campus at Milestone Church for almost 2 years. I've lived my entire life in the Midwest and I was searching for the right church I could call home, experience spiritual family, and grow in my relationship with Jesus after being water baptized in February 2020. My close friend in the DFW area extended an invite for an online service during quarantine. I was so moved and inspired by the message that I continued attending online services every week until I ended up joining an online Small Group, where I received a glimpse of what it was like to experience spiritual family with other disciples of Christ. After spending lots of time praying, I realized that God had called me to move from Illinois to Texas so I could experience spiritual family in person and develop my faith in Jesus with Milestone Church."

Obviously, this is the exception, but it shows that it's possible for people to take their next steps through the online campus.

We use all the means we have to connect people. That's always the goal, whatever environment we're talking about.

Question: Does online have a pastor?

When we first started online church, it was a shared responsibility and we rotated pastors and hosts. What we've discovered is that online church needs what the other campuses need: a dedicated campus pastor.

The campus pastor becomes a consistent face, is able to build connection with the people, offers encouragement, helps people take their next step, provides prayer and counsel, and shares the stories of what God is doing in the lives of people.

And like the other campus pastors, the freedom from having to carry the weight of preparing and preaching every week frees them to be more engaged with their other responsibilities.

Structuring our online church this way provides a whole new environment for new leaders to serve, offer their gifts. It's a win for the whole church.

We're Led by the Spirit

While we do our best to have a detailed growth plan and to wrestle with the strategic questions, we'll always leave room to be led by the Spirit. We try to follow the expansion model of the early church in the book of Acts. Jesus told the disciples in Acts 1:8 that He would give them power to be His witnesses in Jerusalem, in all Judea and Samaria, and then to the ends of the earth.

There was a general plan for expansion, but the Spirit opened unique doors along the way. In Acts 6, they realized they had to restructure their leadership team in order to be more effective. In Acts 10, Peter realized Jesus was sending them to reach everyone, not just the Jewish people. In Acts 15, after they settled some critical theological and discipleship issues, they prayed and sent a bunch of leaders to different places.

And in Acts 16, Paul has a vision of a man from Macedonia who said, "Come over and help us." Without over-spiritualizing it, this is how we started our Haslet campus. Some of the students in our Milestone families who were commuting from Haslet started to invite their friends to church. So many students wanted to come, there weren't enough rides to get them over to Keller.

As a short-term solution we rented a bunch of buses to get them to our Keller campus. But we soon realized God was doing something. So we put the plans in motion to secure a space, prayerfully find a campus pastor, prepare for a launch date, and begin to invite people from our Keller campus to pray about joining a new campus in Haslet.

Because they already believed in reaching people and building lives, making space for new people, and helping others experience what God had done in their lives, hundreds of them agreed to join the team.

But how do we continue to be ready? How do we continue to prepare for the opportunities so we can be led by the Spirit? What's the biggest obstacle standing in our way?

Keep reading and we'll discover it together.

KEY THOUGHTS

- The best explanation for one church in multiple locations: it's the strategy God has given us to continue to expand what God has done in and through us to reach more people and build more lives.

- One church in multiple locations allows more people to use their gifts. When every person in a church engages with the mission of God and uses their gifts to serve people, the church builds itself up in love. What does our broken and hurting world need? More love!

- How do we know how to expand?
    1. We start with a growth plan.
    2. We wrestle with strategic questions.
    3. We're led by the Spirit.

- Why do we use videos at our campuses? It's the best way for us to love and serve people and it allows the majority of resources at our campuses to be directed to connecting with and reaching new people.

- What about church online? We've realized that before most people step foot on one of our physical locations, they will experience us online.

- Two primary functions of online church:
    1. To provide a first impression for all people learning more about Milestone Church

2. To serve as the campus for people who don't live near one of our physical campuses

- In both settings the goal is the same: *reaching people and building lives.* Same vision, different campus.

NEXT STEPS ✓

—The church is healthy, growing, and engaged with the mission of God when everyone uses their gifts to serve others and do their part in the body. If you aren't serving, it's time to jump in and find where God can use your gifts to serve others.

—Do you have a friend, family member, or co-worker who doesn't live near one of Milestone's physical campuses? Invite them to our online campus. It's an easy step to introduce them to spiritual family.

—Pray for our continued growth and expansion at current and future campuses.

13

LEADERSHIP
DEVELOPMENT

OKAY, YOU MADE IT TO THE LAST CHAPTER.
You're probably waiting for the answer to the cliffhanger I left
you with in chapter 12.

And more than give you the answer, we're also joining Jesus in an
important prayer He told us to pray in Matthew 9:38: *Ask God
for more workers!*

We want to grow and expand. We want to be ready to be led by
the Spirit. So what's stopping us? What's the biggest obstacle?

We realize this requires resources and money. God has always
provided more than enough through the generosity, faith, and
obedience of the people of Milestone Church. We're confident
He's going to continue to provide.

We also realize this will require property and real estate in strategic locations. This can be daunting and look impossible—those were the words we heard from the real estate agents when we felt like God wanted us to find 50 acres in Keller. But God provided then, and we believe He'll continue to provide for us.

> **The most important area of need for us as we continue to prepare will be *the leaders who serve in these new locations.***

But more than money or real estate, I believe the most important area of need for us as we continue to prepare will be *the leaders who serve in these new locations.*

You probably figured it out. Naming the chapter "Leadership Development" was a major spoiler.

But whether we realize it or not, the challenge remains. We have to find a way to solve this problem.

Without the leaders we need to serve people and make it possible to reach people and build lives in new areas, none of this growth and expansion will be possible.

It is the critical piece. It is that important.

Let me also be clear: we can't solve this purely with good strategy and a clear goal. We need supernatural help. Jesus tells us we need to pray for these leaders.

In Matthew 9, Jesus went through all the towns and villages of the area preaching, teaching, and healing the sick. He saw the crowds of people and had compassion on them because they were like sheep without a shepherd. He told the disciples, "The harvest is plentiful but the workers are few. Ask the Lord of the harvest, therefore, to send out workers into his harvest field."[1]

When Jesus saw the crowds and the help they needed, He didn't immediately meet their need. He told the disciples they needed to pray and ask God to send more workers. The very next verse (Matthew 10:1) shows Jesus sending out the disciples to do the ministry.

His strategy hasn't changed. He's looking for leaders.

And it's not just any leaders. It's leaders who share our values. It's leaders who are building toward the same goals with the same spirit as part of the same spiritual family. This takes longer, but it's worth it.

Where Will Leaders Come From?

We work with a lot of churches. We help as many as we possibly can because we love the body of Christ. This is the key issue churches are facing. It's not a shortage of vision or opportunities. It's a shortage of leaders. So where do we find them?

① It's you!

If you haven't figured this out yet, one of the primary reasons we spend so much time talking about helping you take your next step is because we believe ministry is not something for the paid professionals. God gives ministry to every believer.

We don't believe every person should leave the marketplace and work for the church. We believe Ephesians 4:11-12 makes

---

[1] Matthew 9:37b-38

it clear this is a smaller group charged with the responsibility of equipping the body of Christ to do ministry. If you're not familiar, verse 11 says that God gave "some" to have specific roles in the church. Verse 12 explains why—in order to equip the saints for the work of the ministry and to build up the body. This word "saint" doesn't mean super-Christians, people who don't make mistakes, or people who have all the answers. It's a simple term referring to anyone in the family of God.

We're all in the game. We all have a contribution to make. We all have a gift to offer and abilities to steward and develop. We all have a measure of leadership.

We could not be more grateful for our hard-working team, but the answer to reaching people and building lives is to equip people to use their gifts, not to hire everyone to work at the church.

If you're a follower of Christ, you're in the ministry. Again, I'm so grateful to be part of a church that understands this. You model it so well. Every weekend it takes thousands of volunteers (across all of our campuses) sacrificing their time so new people can encounter God—often for the very first time.

② Residents and Interns

We're always on the lookout for people with leadership potential who are willing to serve in a role for a developmental season. We make space for residents and interns in all of our departments.

An intern is typically someone who's filling an entry-level role for a shorter duration of time. The goal may be a meaningful experience for a young person in school. We've consistently had interns who were in high school or college and weren't looking for full-time employment but definitely benefited from the leadership development process.

A resident is typically someone with previous work experience and skills who's pursuing long-term placement or employment. Sometimes they grow up in our environment. In other situations, they find us. We're open to either approach because we believe investing in people always helps to advance the Kingdom.

We realize that in our residency we may invest and develop young leaders who God ends up placing in another environment. We trust God and we want to be a blessing to the body of Christ. But we also believe that many of our residents and interns will end up joining our team, and some will become the staff at a new campus.

Ryan

Ryan came to Milestone as a resident. He was engaged to a young lady named Kamalei. They both believed God brought them to Milestone and wanted to become part of our student ministry team. Ryan joined us as a resident, did a great job, and ended up joining our team. After they got married, Kamalei joined the team as well.

Because he enjoyed his experience so much, Ryan told a friend about the residency program.

> Before long, his friend (also named Ryan) became a resident on our Connections team. Once his residency was complete, he ended up joining our team. He also got married—his wife, Ashley, serves on our worship team—and Ryan now serves at one of our campuses.
>
> In case you're wondering, you don't have to be named Ryan to be a resident!

We love young leaders—and leaders who are young at heart! We want to help them grow into everything God has created them to be. We're not called to help all of them, but we do our absolute best to develop every one God sends to us, whether they end up joining our team or not.

While we're passionate about the vision God has given us, we don't think it's better or more important than anyone else's. We don't apologize for who God has called us to be, but we're just grateful to be a small part of God's plan.

We believe in the body of Christ. We believe in the local church. We host equipping events to help churches in our area. A large part of our missions' budget goes toward planting and blessing churches.

③ Milestone College

Maybe you're wondering, *Why would a church start a college?* It's a reasonable question. Typically when we think of higher education in general, there may be a disconnect between that context and the church. It may seem strange.

What's the oldest college in America? Most people know it's also widely considered the most prestigious: Harvard University. Why was it founded? To train clergy, which is another name for pastors. This was not the exception; it was very much the pattern. In fact, roughly 106 of the first 108 colleges were started either by the church or with the expressed purpose of training and developing Christian leaders.

Milestone College is very much in keeping with this tradition. Our desire is to train and develop the next generation of Christian leaders. This is a big step from an internal training program or Bible school. We believe in both of those approaches, but our college is fully accredited through our partnership with Oral Roberts University.

Our goal is to help young leaders pursue their potential call to vocational ministry. We believe many of these students will become future staff and help provide the leadership needed for continued expansion and growth for all of our Milestone campuses.

But this is not the sole purpose of Milestone College. We're trying to match each student with God's unique call for their life and help every one of them take their next step toward God's purpose for their lives—wherever that takes them.

Some of the students will end up serving other churches and advancing the Kingdom of God outside of our environment. We see that as a huge win for them and the body of Christ!

And we also believe some of these students will discover God's plan for their lives by leading outside of vocational ministry. In this case, we believe they will still benefit greatly from the leadership development they receive as they fulfill their early requirements that will transfer with them as they move to a school that offers the degree program they're pursuing.

At the same time, we understand that future campus worship leaders, campus pastors, production, kids ministry, marketing and communication, and online staff members are all waiting to be developed and called to fill key roles on our team.

It takes longer, but it's worth it. We're committed to developing an incredible leadership engine that launches young people into their calling and helps advance God's Kingdom purposes through His Church.

④ Divine Additions

Because we believe God places the members in the body as He sees fit, we're always open to the pieces of the team He chooses to add.

Jeff

For example, one of our pastors, Jeff, was running a company in the marketplace when he first started coming to Milestone. As he continued to move through the Growth Track, understand our values, and look for opportunities to serve, he felt a sense God was calling him to be part of our team. This was no small move, for him or for his family. But after prayerfully considering it, he believed this was more than a career opportunity. He believed God was moving him on the chess board.

> And because he believed this and answered the call, Milestone Church (and all the people it impacts) has been impacted in an incredible way.

Primarily our goal is to empower ministry where God's already placed you but we do realize there are times when God redirects a person's path and gives them a new assignment. We have many team members whose career path took them through the marketplace before landing in ministry, and we're open to these opportunities when God supernaturally adds someone through the mutual sense of the person and our team.

We realize that as people go through the Growth Track and serve in real time in real areas of ministry as volunteers, there will be gifts and callings that emerge.

I think about this daily and spend a lot of time praying about it. I've been thinking and praying about a person who retires around 50, who decides God's next assignment for him is to transition from the marketplace and serve in pastoral care at one of our campuses. He may have been successful in developing resources but he's looking for a greater level of fulfillment. We believe there are opportunities for people in this season to transition into a new role in the Kingdom.

I want to make sure we're doing everything we can to position ourselves to give every person the opportunity to pursue God's plan for their lives.

This probably won't be the biggest track for leadership development, but we do realize it's an important one.

KEY THOUGHTS

- What's the largest obstacle in our expansion? Leaders to serve in our new locations. Without the leaders we need to serve people and make it possible to reach people and build lives in new areas, none of this growth and expansion will be possible.

- The key issue churches are facing? It's not a shortage of vision or opportunities; it's a shortage of leaders—not any leader, but leaders who are building toward the same goals with the same spirit as part of the same spiritual family.

- Where will leaders come from?
    1. It's you!
    2. Residents and Interns
    3. Milestone College
    4. Divine Additions

- Why would a church start a college? To match each student with God's unique call for their life, and to help every one of them take their next step toward God's purpose for their lives—wherever that takes them.

- It takes longer, but it's worth it. We are committed to building a leadership engine to advance the Kingdom of God.

NEXT STEPS

—Leadership is a process. Pray and ask God where He has you in your development. How can you use your gifts to serve others?

—Do you know someone (a friend, co-worker, or relative) who may be a candidate for a leadership environment, such as an internship or even a divine addition? Or who may want to seek an education in leadership/ministry at Milestone College? Encourage them to seek God and take a step.

—Pray and ask God to continue to send leaders to advance the mission He has for Milestone.

CONCLUSION

As this book comes to a close, I'm praying you've found the treasure buried in the field. I hope Jesus has helped you see past the dirt to the incomparable riches we can only find in His Kingdom.

Every time we talk about these things, I see them in a new light. I can't tell you how honored I am to be your pastor. It's such an incredible privilege. I don't take it for granted. Honestly, I'm grateful to be part of the family, no matter what my role is. I am more excited than ever to serve you.

God has given us a clear mission and a clear vision— we're going to reach people and build lives. We're going to join Him in building the only thing He ever promised to build: His Church. I really believe that through Jesus, the local church is the hope of the world. I really believe it's the most resource-rich environment on the planet—not because I'm a pastor, but because I'm a follower of Christ, a husband, a dad, a son, a friend, and because I've experienced the power of it in every aspect of my life.

We have a clear set of values—we believe the Bible, mission, discipleship, spiritual family, and generosity should frame the way we live on a daily basis. We're more committed to these values than ever before. We believe that when we actually live these out by the power of the Holy Spirit, when we can see them reflected in how we live our lives, the impact is undeniable. Not because we're perfect. Not because we don't make mistakes. But because we're all moving toward the same goal and we're making progress.

We have a plan for growth and expansion. How do we respond to the goodness of God? What's the appropriate way for us to show our joy and our gratitude? We want to do for someone else what someone did for us. We want to help as many people as possible experience this treasure buried in a field. No price is too high to pay. No cause is more deserving of our time, our talent, and our treasure.

What am I asking all of us? Quite simply, I'm asking you to continue to be who you are. Be the intentional, authentic, sincere people God has called us to be. Keep loving people. Keep being the hands and feet of Jesus. Keep being the family of God.

We grow and mature into everything God created us to be when each of us does our part. No one can do your part for you. You can't do everything, but you can do your part. Your unique gifts and talents combined with your unique personality create an opportunity for other people to experience the love of God.

Don't ever underestimate how significant your part is. You may not be celebrated, you may not feel like it matters, but God sees every deed and every word done in love in Jesus' name.

Let's take our next step. Because discipleship is one Christ-follower helping another Christ-follower take their next step, we never graduate from the process. As long as we're here, we're taking steps and helping others.

You can't skip steps. You can't take every step all at once, but you can take the next step in front of you. What is God asking of you right now? Don't worry about what's down the road. There will be plenty of time for those steps when the time comes. Let's keep our eyes on the next step, and let's be faithful to keep following Jesus.

Continue to love people. Warmly greet the person sitting next to you. Go out of your way to make them feel seen and loved.

Continue to discover your gifts. Join the Serve Team. You'll make friends and become a better version of the person God created you to be. In case you missed it, the best place to start in this process is our Growth Track.

Continue to serve others. Be on the lookout for Small Group leaders. Think about new projects for Serve Day. Get creative and dream big about how we can impact more people through practical demonstrations of God's love.

Don't stop giving generously—it's making a massive impact in the lives of real people. We truly are one of the most generous churches in the world. It's overwhelming, and I believe it makes

God so proud. We're never more like God than when we're generous.

Here's an inspiring thought: When was the last time you stepped out and did something bold for Jesus? When was the last time you did something by faith—meaning, if God didn't come through, you didn't have a way to make it happen on your own?

Hebrews 11:6 tells us that without faith it's impossible to please God, because those who come to Him must believe He exists and He rewards those who earnestly seek Him. This is another one of those things we never retire from. Let's not allow our natural propensity for safety and security to keep us from stepping out and obeying God, because we trust Him so much.

And finally, let's keep an eternal perspective. Heaven is a real place. Someday we'll be with Him. There will be no sickness. There will be no sorrow. There will be no more evangelism. Nothing will happen outside of God's perfect will. What a day that will be!

But until that day, we have work to do. Hell is a real place. There will be permanent separation from God for those who choose it. Let's try our absolute best to empty hell and fill heaven.

Eternity is a long time. Let's leave nothing in the tank on this side of things.

I'm so proud of you, and I could not be more grateful to be part of this spiritual family.

VISIT US ONLINE

MILESTONECHURCH.COM

ALSO FROM
JEFF LITTLE